2935007

Made in the USA

David Bergmann

TAKE ME TO YOUR
UMLAUTS!

An American goes back
to his German Roots

BLAUPAUSE BOOKS

David Bergmann, born in Ohio in 1971, moved to Germany in 1996 in order to learn the language of his ancestors. After an informative Semester at the Universität Göttingen bankrupted him, he moved to Hamburg, where he now works among a bunch of high-powered, no-nonsense, German business-types.

The awfully cool German Language

What happens when an American has an intensive, upclose encounter with the German language? David Bergmann, in Germany since 1996, has left a long linguistic path behind him, strewn with many a mistake and miscomprehension. Along the way, not only has he learned the difference between a *"möbliertes"* (furnished) room and a *"vermöbeltes"* (thrashed) one, but also why it's sometimes better to address a person using the formal *"Sie"* form instead of with a prematurely personal *"Du"*. In the meantime, he has also mastered (well, almost) the twelve possible plural-forms, and he now realizes that the German translation of "happy ending" is not actually *"Schluß mit lustig"* (that's enough!), but rather "Happy End".

His book is an amusing journey through the German language and a non-native-speaker's remarkable declaration of affection. Translated now into English, this book continues the mission of the original: to convince people of the inherent coolness of the German language – Umlauts and all.

David Bergmann

TAKE ME TO YOUR UMLAUTS!

An American goes back
to his German Roots

BLAUPAUSE BOOKS

To my parents, Margaret and Otmar. More than anyone else, you helped to make this book possible.

Over the years, I have been asked many times what the hardest thing has been for me when it came to writing a book in a foreign language. My reply: that most of my family and friends back home can't read it. It therefore gives me great pleasure to publish this English translation of *"Der, Die, Was? – Ein Amerikaner im Sprachlabyrinth"*. Of course, not every linguistic nuance can survive being translated from German to English, but I nevertheless strongly feel that the spirit of the original version comes shining through.
Besides, here and there I have sprinkled in a new little extra joke or two.

www.umlauts.eu

www.derdiewas.de

www.blaupause-books.com

ISBN 978-3-933498-18-2

© 2012 BLAUPAUSE BOOKS
Originally published under the title DER, DIE, WAS? by David Bergmann
Copyright © 2007 by Rowohlt Verlag GmbH, Reinbek bei Hamburg

Translation: David Bergmann

Layout: Olaf Hille, Hamburg
Cover illustration: Annika Siems, Hamburg

Printed in Denmark

Contents

1: Lovelier at Second Sight 7

2: Germany, "Home of the Umlauts!" 15

3: Coming to Terms with the Past (tense) 24

4: Der, die, WAS?! 32

5: We have Ways of making you talk ... German! 40

6: Sometimes the best Words come in small Packages . . 50

7: We would like some "Fahrvergnügen", please. 58

8: Future (-tense) Shock 66

9: To "ihr" is Human 74

10: Idiosyncratic Idioms 83

11: Textbook-German vs. Colloquial-German 92

12: Reflecting on German Reflective-Verb 101

13: Preferred Prefixes 109

14: One Auto, two "Äuto"? 118

15: German Levity of Brevity 126

16: By your Command! 135

17: Cruel Language? Cool Language! 142

18: Reforming the German Language Reforms 151

19: From "Ami" to "Zoni" 159

20: Confusing Contractions 168

21: How do you "du"? 176

22: Rolling with the German R's 184

23: "Doinglish" 192

24: Chewing through the German CH-Sound 201

25: On a Scale of "So la la" to "Ooh la la!" 210

26: Auf Wiedergucken 218

1: Lovelier at Second Sight

For one special week, I was "*hasenclever*" (bunny clever). I had learned a new German word. One day, almost a year after my move from Chicago to Germany, I saw a street in Hamburg called "*Hasenclever*" street. The word "*bienenfleißig*" (busy as a bee) was already one of my favorite words, but I found "*hasenclever*" to be even more appealing, in fact, almost as attractive as a "*dufte Biene*" (a "hot chick", but literally: "a cute bee").

During the next few days, I enthusiastically applied my new word as often as possible. Everything that I deemed to be more than just clever I now described as being "*hasenclever*". The reactions of the natives varied considerably: Some didn't seem to notice anything unusual, whereas others merely smiled, slightly puzzled, and nodded. Only one German woman admitted to me somewhat skeptically, "Hm. Personally, I've never known bunnies to be all that clever". But I didn't let that confuse me: When it came to the German language, I now felt like I, too, was finally a "wise old bird".

At the time, I shared an apartment with a Swiss fellow by the name of Bodo who was pursuing a doctorate at the University of Hamburg. His dissertation dealt with a medieval manuscript written in Latin. Unlike me, he never seemed to be at wits end with that language, or any dead one for that matter. Fortunately for me, he was also interested in living languages, including the German one which I was trying so eagerly to learn. In our circle of friends, he was aptly referred to as the "*Sprachpfleger*" (language chaperon).

One weekend, Bodo did something which impressed me considerably. As a result, I naturally exclaimed in German something along the lines of: "Hey Bodo, that was clever! That was even '*HASEN-clever*'!" Bodo looked at me for a long while, rather pensively. Then he stated, "*David, man kann entweder klug, geschickt, raffiniert, gerissen, schlau, gewieft, listig, gewitzt, durchtrieben, pfiffig oder sogar clever sein – aber Hasenclever war ein Schriftsteller.*" ("David, in German you can be intelligent, skillful, refined, crafty, shrewd, cunning, sly, wily, scheming, smart, or even clever – but "Hasenclever" was an author.")

Suddenly, I no longer had the impression that I was particularly clever. I thought it was a real shame that my newfound word didn't have the meaning I had thought it had and which had delighted me so over the past week. However, when learning a foreign language, one is bound to have an abundance of disappointing experiences. Fortunately, dozens of funny situations arise as well, many of which, however, only seem comical long afterwards, and often far, far away from the scene of the linguistic crime. Thankfully, I have been keeping a diary for years so that I, too, can sometimes join in the laughter.

Three and a half years previously, on 12 February 1994, I began learning German for fun. And I am still enjoying it to this very day. Over this time, Germans have asked me literally thousands of times how this could possibly be. My absolutely honest answer: Because German is such a beautiful, efficient, important, and, most of all, fun language! If I had received a roll for every skeptical glance I have gotten in reaction to this proclamation, I would now be rolling in it.

In my opinion, unfortunately far too few Germans seem to realize just how humorous their mother tongue really is. I am firmly convinced that they just don't pay enough attention to their own language. For example, the unexpectedly poor election results for Angela Merkel and the CDU in the federal elections of 2005 were a big surprise for many people – but not for me. Although the reason was staring people in the face from just about every street corner, few, if any, Germans appear to have noticed it. The omnipresent posters showed a picture of a smiling Mrs. Merkel next to the CDU election pledge of *"Mehr Arbeit!"* (More work!) This clearly violated a principle of one of the most intelligent Germans of all time, Albert Einstein. This stated: "Everything should be made as simple as possible, but not simpler." Of course, the slogan should rather have been *"Mehr Arbeitsplätze!"* (More employment!) I suspect that many voters registered this subconsciously, and then, due to some vague uneasy feeling, voted against the CDU.

At a closer glance, you can find many similar expressions in German, though not all of them have such grave consequence as in the case above. Some of them are just unintentionally amusing, for example:

- *"Der Mann ist ganz schön hässlich."*
- *"Sie besucht einen Crashkurs gegen Flugangst."*
- *"Dass er das ganze Geld einsackt, kommt bei mir nicht in die Tüte."*

And here the approximate translations:
- "The man is beautifully ugly."
- "She is taking a crash-course on the fear of flying."
- "It's not my bag that he bagged all of the money."

My favorite example is *"Der Mann kriegt seinen Scheiß einfach nicht gebacken"* which directly translates as "The man simply can't get his shit baked." The first time that I heard a colleague say this, I wondered to myself why anyone would ever want to heat up their excrement, little guessing the sentence's true meaning: "The man can't get his crap in order."

Every German knows the saying, *"Deutsche Sprache, schwere Sprache"* (German language, difficult language), but very few Germans realize they could equally correctly declare, *"Deutsche Sprache, spaßige Sprache!"* (German language, fun language!) I find this situation absolutely unacceptable! It's about time for someone to do something about the bad reputation of the German language! Perhaps a very curious American of German descent?

And, coincidentally, I happen to be just such a very curious American of German descent. Hence this book, in which 26 surprisingly painless chapters describe not only what German grammar looks like through a pair of foreign eyes, but also how an American – whose 32 great- great- great-grandparents emigrated from Germany to the U.S. in the middle of the 19th century – goes "back to the roots," both physically as well as linguistically.

This collection of my impressions and experiences is meant to cause people to reconsider their conceptions of the German language, and, even more importantly, to let them laugh while they are doing it. It intends to reveal that German is not at all an awful language, as my fellow countryman Mark Twain once mistakenly wrote, but rather an awfully cool one!

***

As so many things in America do, this story had its actual beginnings on an English emigration ship. As a boy, I was long convinced that my ancestors had come to America on the sailing ship "The Mayflower" in 1617. Admittedly, when it came to my family history, there was a whole series of rather unscientific assumptions that I had taken for granted. For example, there was no doubt in my young mind that my ancestors were among the Puritans who had escaped from religious persecution in England, and then were later among the Puritans who persecuted people of other religions in New England. They also supported George Washington and the English in throwing out the French, and then later they assisted him and the French in throwing out the English. Admittedly, these were some very strange ideas, but then again, at that time I was also fully convinced that Santa Claus, the Easter Bunny, and the Tooth Fairy all convened regularly to coordinate which gifts I should receive.

In contrast to German schools, American schools still teach many positive myths about the founding of the country. For instance, basically every child in the United States knows that the courageous Christopher Columbus discovered "The New World" in 1492, and that since then its northern part has just gotten better and better ever since. However, it is less familiar to most of these pupils that Columbus rather confused the natives by calling them "Indians," constantly inquiring about their gold reserves, wanting to baptize them, and even trying to convince them of the advantages of slave-life. In the United States, people learn to be patriotic at a very young age. Every positive aspect of the country's history is emphasized and we learn that, as Americans, we have somehow all participated in it. At least this was true for me during my childhood. But then, one day, my 3rd grade teacher had a bad cold, and I was robbed of my illusions.

The cultures of Western Civilization are connected not only by the Christian faith, the perceived role of the State, and the consequences of the Enlightenment. An equally elementary link is the fun that children have whenever a substitute teacher takes over the class. It generally means the same for all pupils everywhere: namely no homework, as well as a few unruly, boisterous, and anarchical hours. In my country school a few miles (about 300) southeast of Chicago, we had yet another reason to get excited about substitute teachers. Even though we didn't know exactly why, we quickly noticed that substitutes who didn't come from our area had considerable difficulties pronouncing our last names. During roll-call, they were regularly bewildered by tongue-twisters such as Goettemoeller,

Schwietermann, Thobe, or Knapke. After that, they were usually so demoralized that they only had enough energy left to just go and get the movie projector.

In that particular week in the fall of 1979, however, a new substitute teacher came from especially far away. To our surprise, she did not seem to have any problems at all with our last names. Moreover, after roll-call, she said something that astonished us even more, "Oh, so many beautiful German last names!" We children were flabbergasted. Until then, we were firmly convinced that we had "American" last names. Albeit, we hadn't yet found a name like "Schaeflein" or "Ronnebaum" among the lists of American Presidents, but we still felt one hundred percent American. After this bombshell of a statement, every child in the class raised his or her hand to ask about the origin of his or her last name. Each and every time, the teacher's answer was the same: "Germany!" We were so perplexed that we weren't even capable of whining when she then proceeded to bury us under an enormous amount of homework.

After these shocking realizations, I decided to conduct some genealogical research. When you are eight years old, research basically consists of one thing: asking Dad. My father explained that the substitute teacher must have come from Germany, and that she was indeed right: Almost all of the inhabitants of our town are of German descent. And then came the biggest bombshell of them all: My father explained to me that the gibberish that my Grandmother Bergmann always used with the other elderly ladies of the neighborhood was not a "Secret-Grandma-Language" after all, as I had previously thought, but rather a German dialect called "Low German" or *"Platt-deutsch"*.

Perhaps I should provide some background information about my misconception regarding the Secret-Grandma-

Language. When I was three years old, my grandfather died. Shortly thereafter, my parents purchased from the other heirs the family farm on which my father had grown up. Along with about 120 acres of land (approximately 45 hectares), this included a farmhouse containing all sorts of odds and ends, among other things my Grandmother Bergmann. With us she only spoke English, but as soon as another gray-haired woman came along, a miraculous transformation occurred. She immediately stopped whatever she was doing (such as finding work for any lazy grandchildren lounging around), and switched languages. One moment, we were able to understand everything, and then the next, nothing at all. In my childish ignorance, I believed that it was a Secret-Grandma-Language spoken by grandmothers throughout the world to prevent grandchildren from catching on to what they were plotting.

I even had some written proof for my theory. This could be found both at the local cemetery and in the local church, two common gathering places in my town for the grandmothers. In both places, there was a secret written language in mysterious letters. (Not until many years later would I discover that the texts on the gravestones were not actually Grandma Résumés, nor those on the church walls Grandma Commandments: They were just typical church matters written in the old German *"Fraktur"* script.)

At the age of eight, kids are not yet capable of doing much serious research. But instead of giving up completely, I just took a break for a few decades. Much later, I discovered that most of the inhabitants of my village did indeed have German ancestors. They had originated from the region between Osnabruck and Bremen and came to the USA during the 1830s and 1840s.

America has long been described as a melting pot, and there is a lot of truth to that. In the cities, the ethnic groups tend to quickly assimilate: The first generation may prefer to stay among themselves in their own part of town, but in the second generation the lads and lassies from different immigrant groups are much more prone to mixing and mingling. As is often the case, however, things could be very different in our neck of the woods in the countryside. Here, the so-called melting pot simmered for a very long time indeed.

In my home area, for instance, for many decades few non-German speakers dared to move to a town in which everyone seemed to know everyone else, all strangers were distrusted, and just about everyone spoke Low-German (and not only the grandmothers, as was to be the case in later generations). Not until the influence of radio, TV, and two World Wars with decidedly un-happy-endings for Germany made themselves felt was Low-German finally forced to give way to English.

And not even the clever Grandmas could stop that.

2: Germany, "Home of the Umlauts!"

It was once upon a time in the United States. A new, exclusively expensive brand of ice cream suddenly appeared on the ice cream scene. Nobody knew exactly where it had come from. There were many rumors floating around: Denmark? Holland? Iceland? Of course, Iceland's name alone would have sufficed to be an appropriate homeland for such a frozen delicacy…

The epicenter of all of this sweet speculation was the ice cream brand "Häagen Dazs". Not until much later would large swathes of the populace learn the truth about this ice cream's origin. To the disappointment of many American ice cream connoisseurs, it was revealed that the producer was just a run of the mill American from New York. Instead of originating from some Nordic language, the name was simply an artistic term which was supposed to look and sound European to the American consumers and be associated with European tradition and craftsmanship. But, by this time, it was too late: The ice cream brand's whiff of European flair could no longer be snatched away from it.

It is difficult for native English speakers to understand why umlauts aren't properly appreciated in the languages in which they appear. For example, a Swedish friend of mine from Hamburg with the last name Källner wanted to get rid of her umlaut simply because she believed that with it, her last name didn't appear international.

On the other hand, American and British hard rock bands have long been aware of the umlauts' "cöölness". They realize that umlauts give band names a "foreign-ish" appearance and even seem to imply a certain "mythical Germanic toughness." The random umlaut in rock music was introduced by Blue Öyster Cult and later adopted by Motörhead and Mötley Crüe. The graphic designer who designed the cover of

Motörhead's first album created the so-called "hard-rock-umlaut". "We did it simply because it looks nasty," commented the singer. Supposedly, the umlauts in Mötley Crüe stemmed from the members' favorite drink, Löwenbräu.

All of these examples make it easy to accuse native English speakers of having a certain degree of umlaut-envy. After all, the English language does not have the cute letters Ä, Ö, and Ü. We didn't even have a name for them in English, so we had to steal the German name "umlaut." Otherwise, they would probably have to be called something like "the two cute alphabetical dots" or "little bird feet." However, at least during its adoption into English it has been given a different plural: "umlauts". (In German, the plural form is inexplicably "Umlaute".)

Of course, German is not the only language in the world in which these little "power dots" appear. You can also find umlauts in languages such as Finnish, Swedish, and Turkish. However, German is in fact the mother of all umlauts. Sometime during the Middle Ages in the German-speaking countries, scribes began writing the letter E over the letter U whenever the combination UE appeared in a manuscript. This was not only a handwriting shortcut, but also space-saving and somehow more elegant. Gradually, the E became smaller and smaller until it finally developed into two dots. Of course, this development was noted by other northern and central European countries and was adopted in many other languages.

At that time, the Arabic script was still used in the rapidly expanding Ottoman Empire. I believe the true reason why the Turks fought their way so fanatically to the gates of Vienna in the 17th century was that they were searching for the "Secrets of the Umlauts". But since they were repulsed by the Austrians, the written Turkish language was to remain "umlautless" for several additional centuries. The Latin script – along with umlauts – was not introduced to the Turks until shortly after World War I. (I suspect that in return for their military support of the German and Austrian empires in the Great War, the Turks demanded umlaut secrets. And they got them!) Umlauts pose two general problems for English native speakers. First, how are they supposed to be pronounced? Second, when do they appear? The importance of these questions should not be underestimated! After all, these dots can lead to significant differences in meaning, as is demonstrated by the following sentences:

- "Ich *zähle, während du zahlst.*" – (I'll **count** while you **pay**.)
- "Manche Leute werden *geachtet, andere geächtet.*" – (Some people are **respected**, whereas others are **ostracized**.)
- "Der Bischof redete von *schwülen Tagen, der Bürgermeister hingegen von Schwulen.*" – (The bishop spoke of **humid** days; whereas the mayor spoke of **gays**.)

When it comes to native English speakers learning German, the umlauts challenge (*"fordern"*) rather than assist (*"fördern"*). In this respect, the umlauts could be called the skunks of the language world: cute from a safe distance but potentially problematic the closer you get to them.

When native English speakers begin learning German, most of them don't really know how an umlaut should sound. That is why the so-called "hard-rock-umlauts" don't actually effect the pronunciation of the bands' names. One of my German grammar books stated it this way: "The exact pronunciation of umlauts cannot be expressed in writing. These simply must be learned in the language lab". The book also just pointed out the following examples: a long Ä as in *"Hähne"* (roosters), a short Ä as in *"Hände"* (hands), a long Ö as in *"Öfen"* (oven), a short Ö as in *"öffnen"* (to open), a long Ü as in *"grün"* (green), and a short Ü as in *"Gründe"* (reasons). The tongue-twisters which we repeatedly subjected to in the language lab were rather droll. For example: *"Tut die gute Pute in die Blütentüte!"* (Put the good turkey in the bag of blossoms!) and *"Eine Kuh macht Muh, viele Kühe machen Mühe"* (One cow says moo; many cows make trouble).

Admittedly, for a long time I was uncertain whether my German language skills *"blühten"* (blossomed) or rather *"bluteten"* (bled). After a while I somehow managed to approximate the pronunciation of the long umlauts, but I seemed to have considerably less success with the short ones. No matter how hard I tried, I was simply not capable of orally differentiating between *"drücken"* (to press) and *"drucken"* (to print). Most of the time, I just did my best to somehow avoid the problem altogether (*"mich um das Problem herumdrücken"*), not at all an easy task.

The second problem with umlauts in German is knowing when they should be used. For instance, I often found myself wondering whether the German word for congratulation was *"Glückwunsch"*, *"Gluckwünsch"* or *"Glückwünsch?"* Therefore, for a long time I simply played it safe and stuck with the plural form of *"Glückwünsche"* (congratulations). I was also unsure whether my doing laundry was *"wasche Wäsche"* or *"wäsche Wasche."* The following German sentence demonstrates just how randomly umlauts sometimes seem to appear: *"Der Franzose hat keinen Umlaut, spricht dafür Französisch fröhlich mit seiner Frau – einer Französin froher Natur, natürlich – aber wenn er dies mit dem Telefon macht, wird trotzdem nicht teleföniert!"* (The Frenchman has no umlaut, but likes to speak merrily with his wife, a French woman of a cheery nature, of course, but when he does this on the telephone, he still doesn't "telephöne"!)

In spite of all of this, I just can't remain angry at the umlauts for very long. They are simply too adorable. My favorites are the small "ü" which looks like a smiley and the small "ö" which resembles a singing smiley! An English comedian once explained the popularity of umlauts among native English speakers as follows: "It's almost as if they had two eyes. You look at the umlaut, and the umlaut looks right back at you! I believe that, because of the umlauts, a close friendship can arise between the reader and the text being read."

***

When I moved to Chicago in January 1994 in order to start my career in the exciting world of auditing and accounting, of course I thought about umlauts occasionally, but no more than the majority of American men. During my first few weeks there, I was more preoccupied with my having few friends and even fewer pieces of furniture. Finding furniture was clearly the easier of the two tasks. On one cold February evening in 1994, I spotted a flyer hanging in the Laundromat in the basement advertising a moving sale at a nearby apartment on the following weekend.

I was the very first person to knock on the apartment door at the moving sale. A pretty, young American woman opened the door and greeted me with a cheerful, "Hello, my name is Kerry." She asked me what I was looking for, and I told her that since I was new in the city, I didn't have much of anything. She then said something which changed my life: "Oh, then you must be lonely. Why don't you go out to the bars tonight with my friends and me?" In retrospect, I must admit that her marketing technique was very effective, because after that I bought everything she put in front of me. Within a mere few minutes I bore a strong resemblance to a pack-mule.

Not once did I hesitate during my buying spree until she

pulled out a German textbook. Kerry continued to smile, but for once this alone did not convince me of the desirability of the product. I told her that, at age 22, I was definitely too old to learn a foreign language. This caused her smile to broaden even further as she replied, "David, the Germans have an appropriate word for almost everything. One of them fits your statement just perfectly: the word *"Quatsch"*. Its best translation is 'nonsense' but it conveys oh so much more." As a sort of a bulk discount, she then just gave me the book, and I trudged home with all my new acquisitions.

As planned, I went out to the bars with Kerry and her friends that evening. Within the course of the evening, I took an opportunity to ask one of them all about Kerry. She explained that Kerry had lived in Germany for a year where she had met her fiancé, whom she planned to marry next year in Germany. At first, I was disappointed that this captivating woman was already firmly in a German's clutches. But my disappointment did not last for long, because Kerry made me an irresistible offer that same evening: "David, if you speedily work through the textbook, then you can have a dance with me at my wedding in Leipzig next year!"

Even though I was a passionate non-dancer at the time, this offer intrigued me. I decided to give my somewhat involuntarily acquired textbook a chance after all. Upon waking the next morning, I opened the book for the first time. After working through the first few pages, I realized that I could actually learn the material. This was by no means something which I took for granted!

I had had two years of German in highschool in the 80's, but my fellow pupils and I never managed to get very far with it. German seemed very difficult and unimportant to us then, in spite of the abundance of umlauts. To top it all off, our German textbooks were rather ridiculous: hardcore 70's material clearly targeted at the so-called "Woodstock-Generation" (In Germany, referred to as the *"die '68er"*). After two years with these works of art, we were convinced that the entire youth of Germany must have long hippy-hair and think only about parties. In four semesters, I was only able to muster a vocabulary of about a hundred words. Even more embarrassing was that this consisted mostly of party phrases such as, *"Ich heiße David. Bist du auch neu hier?"* (My name is David. Are you also new here?) and *"Ja, ich mag Bier auch sehr."* (Yes, I also like beer very much.)

Working through the first chapter of the book, however, I suddenly realized that I had actually learned how to study hard during my university years. The exercises in Kerry's textbook still caused me some trouble, but at least they were no longer seemingly impossible. Furthermore, over the years since my first failed attempt I also had gotten a very different impression of the German language.

In 1987, I got my driver's license, something which awakened my interest in cars. Soon thereafter, I discovered that VW, BMW, Audi, Mercedes Benz, AND Porsche all come from the same country, thereby increasing my respect for it considerably. Maybe it was then that I first suspected that knowing German could be a very moving experience.

In 1988, the movie "Die Hard" opened in theaters. Ever since Berlin stopped being a serious rival for Hollywood back in the 1930s, many of the best villains in American movies have been German. In "Die Hard", "Raiders of the Lost Ark", "Goldfinger", and many other great movies of my youth, the bad guys were Germans. And to us American youngsters, they were not only evil and cold, they were also evil and cool. This was further proof that understanding German could be cool.

In 1989, four fantastic "Fräuleins" from Bonn visited our highschool for a month. I then realized that some of the most captivating women in the world are German. The four exchange students left a lasting impression on me. I found them cultured, elegant, and fashionable. To me, these "Bonn-Girls" were even better than the "Bond-Girls"! I wanted to talk to them, but words kept failing me. After a few weeks I finally mustered up enough courage. Since I wanted to impress them, I tried to introduce myself in German. Unfortunately, my attempt was somewhat off-target, as I ended up saying *"Ich heißer David. Wie heiß sind Sie?"* ("I'm hot David. How hot are you?"). As they say, close only counts in horseshoes and hand grenades, and in this case I definitely bombed it. I think it was probably for the best that I wasn't able to understand her response. In any event, I never got an opportunity for a second question. Until then, the German language had only been an abstract subject for me, similar to philosophy, history, or mathematics. Now I had another good reason to believe that speaking German could be fantastic.

In 1990, the song "Wind of Change" by the German rock band "Scorpions" became an international hit. For years, the best rock music station in my area had been playing many songs by the Scorpions, but from then on, the Scorpions singer Klaus Meine did commercials for them. His rocky German accent really impressed us American guys every time his voice boomed out from the radio: "WTUE, the station where the Scorpions rock you like a HURRICANE!" Here was yet a further argument to assume that boning up on German could be rocking.

In 1991, our local TV station aired a documentary on the small country with large amounts of mountains, tidiness, cheese holes, and bank secrets. It was reported therein that the country's main language was, in fact, not "Swiss", as many Americans mistakenly presume, but rather German. Yet another reason to think that mastering German could pay handsome dividends.

In 1992, I began my minor in history in college. During the course of my studies, I noticed how many of the more interesting figures of world history were German. Also, some of the students in my history courses had a decided advantage over me because they had already studied foreign languages. Again, this furthered my conviction that studying German could be really smart.

In 1993, I read "Flowers for Algernon", a novella about a mentally handicapped man named Charlie who, after undergoing a revolutionary operation, turns into a genius. Unfortunately, the change is not permanent, and at the end of the story – much to the regret of the persons involved – Charlie reverts to his former state. However, at the peak of his intellectual abilities, Charlie is able to read scientific texts in German. When he finally realizes how quickly he is losing his abilities, he tries in vain to reread the German books he had previously found so helpful. Now I was even more certain that knowing German could be absolutely brilliant.

In 1994, I moved to Chicago. Until then, I had still somewhat doubted my father's tales about the German ancestors in my home area. In Chicago, however, these tales sounded more suddenly decidedly more believable. This was because here – in contrast to where I had grown up – there seemed to be a decided minority of tall, white, blond people with German last names. Now, I was firmly convinced that speaking German could be colossal!

As such, after one morning with the German textbook in February 1994, I had developed a new passion: the German language. Or as I like to phrase it: German, the language with umlauts and oh so much more!

3: Coming to Terms with the Past (-tense)

It may be open to debate nowadays whether Germans still have problems coming to terms with their past, but there is no doubt that students of German have considerable difficulties dealing with the German language past-tense.

This is especially true for Asians trying to tangle with the Teutonic tongue. For example, it often happens that a Chinese person says something along the lines of: *"Ich sage zu viel gestern."* (I say too much yesterday.) This occurs because Chinese only has one verb tense, which is modified by various adjectives. Actually, a Chinese person could claim that his grammatical mistake is not so bad, since the meaning of the sentence is clear on account of the time specification. He is correct about that, but it sounds strange nonetheless. It is definitely easier for us as native English speakers. For example, I would never be tempted to say: *"Ich falle letzte Woche bei der Sprachprüfung durch."* (Last week I fail the language exam.)

Furthermore, there is something which makes dealing with the German past-tense easier for native English speakers: The construction of the past perfect, which is especially tormenting for Asians, is done almost the same way in both English and German.

Nevertheless, "easier" is not the same as "easy." Like almost all German students, native English speakers also have difficulties choosing between the simple past and past-perfect-tenses. In both English and German, the past-perfect-tense is used when an act begins in the past and continues into the present. However, this is where the similarities end. If an American, for example, wants to say that he still lives in a city, he would not say, "I am living in this city since five years", but rather "I have lived in this city for five years". This is confusing for Germans, however, as they say it the first way: *("Ich wohne seit fünf Jahren in dieser Stadt"*).

But this is only a minor problem. What really complicates matters in German is that the choice between the two is often simply a question of "style". My grammar book explains it as follows: "As a rule, use the past-perfect-tense when speaking, but use the simple-past-tense when writing." Personally, this doesn't strike me as being particularly stylish.

I have often noticed that foreigners who had not studied German before coming to Germany are more likely to have problems with the simple-past-tense. For example, my friend Juri, a Russian who learned German on the streets of Germany, condescendingly described the simple-past-tense as "Fairy-tale German." I myself prefer the simple-past-tense, since it better approximates the English way of speaking and can often just be spoken faster. After all, why say, *"Ich **bin** gestern über die Straße **gegangen"*** (I have crossed the street yesterday), when I can use fewer syllables and still state just as much, *"Ich **ging** gestern über die Straße"* (I crossed the street yesterday)?

Evidently, even Shakespeare must have dealt with the German language because his famous question, "To be or not to be?" is very relevant when forming the German past-tense (*"Sein oder nicht sein?"*). In modern English, this is never a "matter of be-ing", but it is in German. Kerry's grammar book stated, "Verbs with the helping verb *'sein'* (to be) usually describe a movement from one point to another or a change of conditions." However, this only happens when the verb doesn't have a direct object, as in the following sentence, *"Ich **bin** nach Hamburg **gefahren**, wo ich mich total **verfahren habe"**.* (Directly translated: "I am driven to Hamburg where I have totally lost my way.")

Although I found this to be complicated enough, it became even more difficult. According to the book, some verbs take either *"sein"* (to be) or *"haben"* (to have) as a helping verb, such as *"laufen"* (running), *"fahren"* (driving), *"fliegen"* (flying), and *"schwimmen"* (swimming). For example, *"Otto **hat** den BMW durch den Tierpark **gefahren** und **ist** mit ihm gegen einen mit Affen und Äpfeln ausgestatteten Baum **gefahren**."* (Otto **has driven** the BMW through the zoo and **is driven** into a tree full of apes and apples). The decision about which helping verb to use depends on what you want to emphasize. In this example, the main focus is first placed on the operation of the wagon and then on the tree full of apes and apples. (All of this seemed beastly complicated to me…)

At least I can now understand why the verb *"sein"* (to be) uses *"sein"* as its helping verb. (After all, everyone is happiest among their own kind – in German: *"seinesgleichen"*.) Still, what I don't understand is where the action or change of condition is supposed to be in the sentence: *"Ich **bin** da geblieben und nichts **ist** geschehen."* (I **am stayed** there and nothing **is happened**.)

However, I was somewhat comforted during my early struggles with the German past-tense rules by following the statement in Kerry's grammar book: "For Germans, the way of forming the past-tense in English is practically 'unlearnable'."

***

After a few weeks of intensive study with Kerry's grammar-book gift, I realized I could actually learn German. However, it was equally obvious to me that I would not be able to speak German fluently after working through just one single book. So I decided to improve my German knowledge by going on a vocabulary hunt. I assumed that the best place to find words would be the city library, since it had a large selection of German books. Unfortunately, many of these were so old that they were still printed in the old *Fraktur* script, and many of the "newer" ones dealt primarily with coming to terms with Germany's past during the immediate post-WWII years. Neither of these facts simplified my mission.

As a result, I bought a selection of new books from several different stores. I was disappointed to note that some contained typos in them, such as the bilingual book *"Novellen aus Wein"* (Novellas made of Wine). You would never have guessed from the title that the book contained short stories about the capital of the Danube Dual Monarchy, *"Wien"* (Vienna), at the turn of the century.

My search for more German vocabulary even lead me into church. At that time, some church services in Chicago were still held in German. Unfortunately, at the Sunday service which I attended, only three people were in attendance: the priest, an elderly lady, and me. Even though the lady looked like she had been a contemporary of Bismarck's, I spoke to her after the service. I perceived that she was somewhat hard of hearing, because whenever I tried to say something to her in German, she shook her head and apologized that her English was so bad. At least, I hoped she was hard of hearing...

Since my move to Chicago, I had lived in a very modest apartment where the monthly rent was correspondingly cheap. During my first few days, it seemed to me that I was perhaps just about the only native-born American there. I had the impression that the dwelling housed more nationalities than many UN buildings. The first person I met there was a thirty-something Croatian who, though he could barely speak any English, knew German very well. Since my active German vocabulary at that time consisted primarily of party phrases, his first impression of my personality may have been a slightly distorted one. But as his English and my German slowly improved over the weeks, our conversations became somewhat less monotonous.

Once during my first week in Chicago, I ran into my

Croatian neighbor in the hallway just as he was talking loudly to the landlord in German, Croatian, and Russian. Although I didn't understand what he was trying to communicate, it was obvious that the landlord's response to his questions only annoyed the Croat. The landlord's had namely the same answer to each question, *"Yo no comprendo Español."* Although the U.S. is indeed a country of immigration, many Americans are at a loss on how to react when confronted with people who can't speak any English. In such a case, everything foreign sounds Spanish to them. And, for many Americans, the only solution in such a situation is simply to speak louder.

The landlord was very friendly, but he looked like he hadn't been dusted off since the '70s. I was having a conversation with him at the reception desk one day when a Mexican tenant came along to complain about something. Although he spoke much better English than the Croat, he couldn't think of the appropriate words for his problem. In despair, he ended his English sentence in Spanish with the following words, *"La cucaracha! La cucaracha!"* Perhaps the landlord was seriously concerned with the problem, but the dance he thereupon performed conveyed a slightly different impression. The tension in the room seemed to increase dramatically, and not just on account of all of the dust that had been kicked up...

Much to my regret, I discovered shortly thereafter that cock-roaches were not such a laughing matter after all. When I moved in, I thought I would be living alone. I soon learned otherwise. My first indication was while I was preparing dinner and the telephone rang. In my ignorance, I left my sandwich on the counter unattended. When I came back, I caught a glimpse of it disappearing through a small hole in the wall. Even worse was the tiny note which the cockroaches had left behind, written in all capital letters: "Next time, Country Boy, take it easy on the ketchup." Moreover, I also quickly learned that the lights should be turned on BEFORE getting up to go to the bathroom. It's hard to fall back to sleep after squishing a few cockroaches between your toes. YUCK!

This scream of horror which I sometimes let out during the night was similar to one that came from the foreign language section of a Chicago video store one weekend: "Oh no! Not Gérard Depardieu again!" As I paid for my movie, the man at the cash register leaned over to his startled colleague, who was looking in the direction of the screams, and murmured: "Probably just another college student from the German-Studies program." I found it comforting that I wasn't the only one who felt that way...

Evidently, I had just borrowed the video-store's last German-language VCR-tape which had nothing to do with either the Holocaust or World War II. Unfortunately, the selection in this category was extremely slim. To my surprise, I had read in a German textbook shortly before that Berlin had been one of Hollywood's toughest competitors in the '20s, almost matching the Californian "Dream Factory" film for film. The textbook explained, however, that this had happened a long, long, long time ago. Nowadays, Hollywood definitely may have its problems, but fierce competition from Berlin is certainly not one of them.

While searching for new sources in my endeavor to learn the German language, I discovered that Chicago's video stores carried a lot more French movies than German ones, even if only the ones with Gérard Depardieu in the starring role were counted. In addition, most German movies, such as *"Das Boot"* (The U-Boot) and *"Die Blechtrommel"* (The Tin Drum), had to do with World War II in some form or another. And of these only very few had the required happy-endings. (To be honest, I hadn't expected this kind of having to come to terms with the past ...)

Searching for more German sources, I also found a Chicago radio station with German programming. Most of the songs they played were not even all that bad, but it was not until much later that I found out that many of them weren't actually even sung by Germans. It now seems odd to me that I learned a lot of German from Roger Whittaker, David Hasselhoff, Milva and Howard Carpendale, but I liked their songs better than those sung by Germans on that station. After all, many of those were somewhat silly tunes dating all the way back to the '30s, '40s, and '50s, such as *"Weiße Taube, brauner Bär"* (White Dove, Brown Bear) by Gus Backus.

In the summer of 1994, I discovered a German *"Stammtisch"* (a regular get-together for people interested in a particular thing). Not only were there many Germans, but also other Europeans who could speak German so well that I thought they were Germans. Nobody mistook me for a German, however, not even for a person who understood German. The very first question posed to me caused me to stumble: A woman asked me, *"Gibst du mir bitte das Besteck?"* (Would you please pass me the silverware?) My confused expression and my answer, *"Ick nickt verstehen, was dieser Besteck ist?"* (I not understands what this 'silverwares' is?) did not encourage her to make any further requests of me. Neither the white dove nor the brown bear had prepared me for any of this…

One helpful German noticed how little I was speaking and gave me the following advice, *"David, du musst einfach sprechen!"* (David, you must simply speak!) I thought to myself, "If I speak at all, then it will indeed only be 'simply'!" and remained silent. Not until much later did I realize what he had actually meant. Germans obviously think, owing to their own experiences with speaking English, that you simply need to get rid of your inhibitions and start chatting away. Clearly, they forget that they have already studied English for many years, and, therefore, have a large passive vocabulary at their disposal. However, such a linguistic reservoir is exactly what is missing if you're just beginning to learn German as an American. Therefore, asking a person to "simply speak" German is somewhat like forcing a novice piano player up onto stage in front of a large audience in the hope that this will compensate for his having hardly ever touched a piano previously.

If this discovery were not discouraging enough, I concluded that one shouldn't address girls at American parties with statements like: "Yeah, baby, you heard right. I like to spend my free time with the subtleties of German grammar." Their reactions to this were more devastating than the German post-war movies. In such a situation not even Gerard Depardieu would have stood a chance.

I finally realized that if I wanted to master the past-tense and other forms of the German language, I needed more than just a few textbooks and movies. I needed to take a course which would get me back on course.

4: Der, die, WAS?!

That is THE question. Obviously, students of the German language have many other queries, but the question *"Der, die, was?!"* (The, the, what?!) is THE paramount question.

Native German speakers will probably never really understand how ornery the 'three Musketeers' of *"der"*, *"die"* and *"das"* can be. (These are, respectively, the masculine, feminine and neuter forms of the English word "the".) After all, Germans already complain enough about noun genders when they learn French, Spanish or Italian. And in these languages, there are only two genders to choose from, masculine and feminine. That is only half as difficult! Besides, in these languages the different genders seem to respect each other's boundaries, as genders ought to do. And in these languages, as with people, it is usually easy to guess a noun's gender at first sight.

In English, it is even easier to guess the correct gender. After all, there is only one to choose from! What can go wrong there? This is, however, not the case in German, much to the dismay of all those not raised among them. Normally, there is simply no avoiding having to memorize them.

In my first German grammar books, the information concerning "the battle of the sexes in German" was only helpful to a certain extent. The first book explained things as follows: "The most effective method is to memorize the gender with every new word." Well, this piece of advice is almost as helpful as the following one for students of English: "If you want to know how a word should be pronounced in English, it would be advisable to remember the pronunciation of a new word." Unfortunately, there were no hints for people without photographic memories. The second book recommended: "You have to memorize the genders of the nouns." This statement was not very comforting, but at least it was honest. The third book simply stated: "The genders of German nouns are hard to memorize." This was even less comforting, but at least you clearly knew where you stood.

From other grammar books I gathered together as much useful information as possible on this subject. One rule stated: "All words ending in *'-heit'* or *'-keit'* are feminine, for example, *'Dummheit'* (stupidity), *'Abhängigkeit'* (dependence), and *'Ärgerlichkeit'* (irksomeness)." Another rule was: "Words that end with *'-e'* are mostly feminine, such as *'Frage'* (question), *'Lüge'* (lie), and *'Pappnase'* (fool)." I was pleased about this information, at least until I came across a few exceptions. Not only was I in danger of losing *"das Interesse"* (interest), but also *"der Glaube"* (faith) in the language.

And if this isn't already complicated enough, some German nouns appeared to be a 'transsexual'! These gender-benders can be particularly tricky. Examples include: *"die Kiefer"* (the pine tree) and *"der Kiefer"* (the jaw), *"der Schild"* (the shield) and *"das Schild"* (the sign), as well as *"die Kunde"* (the tidings) and *"der Kunde"* (the customer). A silly sample sentence is as follows: *"Da der Messer sein Messer holte, holte der Leiter seine Leiter"* (When **the** surveyor got **his** knife, **the** leader got **his** ladder). What a dilemma! Or perhaps this should more accurately be referred to as a "trilemma"…?!

Especially frustrating are the synonyms with different genders. Before a meal, for example, you receive a menu on a piece of paper. But this paper could either be called *"der Zettel"* (the piece of paper), *"die Seite"* (the page), or *"das Blatt"* (the sheet). And the food you then receive is either *"der Nährwert"* (the nutritional value), *"die Nahrung"* (the food), or *"das Nahrungsmittel"* (the foodstuff). Then at the end of the meal, the sweet dish you are served can be referred to as either *"der Nachtisch"* (the dessert), *"die Nachspeise"* (the dessert), or *"das*

Dessert" (the dessert). This grammatical complexity threatened to give me a slight case of indigestion…

To top it off, the gender used can also have a significant impact on the meaning of the sentence. After all, there is a clear difference between *"Der macht die Musik"* (He makes the music) and *"Die Macht der Musik"* (The power of music). Now that is what I call power!

In my opinion, these German 'gender battles' culminate in the choice between *"der See"* (the little sea) and *"die See"* (the big sea). Even Germans sometimes have problems differentiating between the two. They may know that *"die Ostsee"* (the Baltic Sea) lies in the north and *"der Bodensee"* (Lake Constance) in the south, but it is more difficult to know the articles of less familiar seas in other countries. Someone told me that the gender generally depends on the size of the body of water. Fortunately, this form of "trans-gendering" only applies to the word *"See"* and not with every masculine word. For example, if *"der Mann"* (the man), *"der Baum"* (the tree), or *"der Streit"* (the argument) all suddenly became feminine as they grew in size, then that mountain (*die Berg*) of German grammar would simply be insurmountable.

What is more, there is basically no getting around this issue in everyday German. If you don't know if a word is masculine, feminine, or neuter, then there is just not very much that you can do with it. Whoever doesn't believe me should simply try to construct a few sentences without using any articles, be they definite or indefintite. At best, you will sound like someone who has just imigrated from a Slavic country, like the proverbial Polish plumber: *"Sie haben Problem mit Toilette in Wohnung? Für Sie habe ich Termin in erste Woche nach übernächstem Vollmond."* (You have problem with toilet in apartment? I have appointment for you in first week after next full moon).

At worst, you simply won't be understood at all. The only

possible solution I have found up until now is to put a diminutive *"-chen"* or *"-lein"* at the end of every noun. These little suffixes namly ALWAYS change the gender of a noun to neuter. (Thank goodness!) Unfortunately, this *"Alternativchen"* (little alternative) is only a short-term solution, as the natives usually start getting suspicious after I have used too many *"Wörtchen"* (little words) in *"Sätzchen nach Sätzchen"* (little sentence after little sentence).

Not even the names of countries in German offer a refuge. In German you find *"die Türkei"* (Turkey) and *"der Irak"* (Iraq), but also *"die Schweiz"* (Switzerland) and *"der Sudan"* (Sudan). Also, you can never be sure if an article is necessary for countries, such as *"die Tschechei"* (the Czech Republic) or *"Tschechien"* (Czech Republic). And even if you do choose the correct article, people might still look at you strangely. I experienced this when I sent a letter to Switzerland and wrote *"Die Schweiz"* (Switzerland) on the bottom of the envelope. The workers at the post office found this simply adorable.

***

In the fall of 1994, I turned to the Chicago Goethe-Institut in order to obtain help with these and other grammar-related problems. The decision was rather easy for me: the inner-city location was first-rate, the staff seemed Teutonically efficient, and a wide selection of courses were being offered. I chose a four-week intensive course which met three hours a day, four days a week.

During the registration, I asked the American who worked at the Goethe-Institut if students of German can hope to ever master the three perfidious pronouns *"der"* *"die"* and *"das"*. After all, to me she seemed to speak perfect German. She replied: "No. I have been learning German for many years now, and I still make lots of mistakes with the articles. I may correctly say *'das Kabel'* (the cable) 99 times, but then, for some inexplicable reason, I mistakenly say, "I need *'einen Kabel'* ("cable" in the masculine form). It's all very vexing!" She continued: "You will always make mistakes with the three articles. This phenomenon is comparable to the scientific experiment of trying to reach absolute zero. You can spend a lot of money and make an enormous effort, but you can only get closer to your goal. You will never actually reach it."

Before the German course began, I had considered myself to already be a hard worker when it came to studying. But there I learned the meaning of true discipline. Our teacher was a friendly but firm man. However, he was so strict that you needed a great deal of courage to endure his displeasure when you had not worked hard enough. Those of us in the class thought "Herr Hartmut" (loosely translated as "Mr. Hard-Courage") was an appropriate name for him. After many years of futile attempts to teach the German language to hopelessly untalented Americans, he had apparently lost a great deal of his patience. I don't know what worried me more: how he angrily growled when I didn't do 110% of my homework or how he dropped his face into his hands, sobbing, after I had read a paragraph out loud with the strongest American accent since John F. Kennedy's famous speech in Berlin in 1963.

The first evening, we had to introduce each other in German. When my turn came, I started to sputter and stutter. With a slight growl, Herr Hartmut said to me, *"Herr Bergmann, Sprechen Sie sich aus!"* (Mr. Bergmann, express yourself clearly!) That was easier said than done. Finally, with an enormous amount of effort, I managed to do it. After the entire class had introduced itself, Herr Hartmut said: "I am pleased to get to know all of you and to have you in this course. Herr Bergmann, go to the library during the first break and check out several cassettes and books on pronunciation!"

There were eight people in the course. Most of us were Americans, and we were interested in the German language for a variety of reasons. The only exotic exception was Paola from Venezuela. Her wealthy father had sent her to America to learn English and to get an education. When Herr Hartmut then asked her how she had ended up at the Chicago Goethe-Institut, she explained: "After several months here in this country, I proudly told my father over the telephone that I could finally speak English very well. I asked him then if I could please return home. His answer was, 'I am proud of you, little daughter. Stay there and learn German now.'" She sighed pensively and added, "My father is a little strict."

When studying languages, like most people, I find memorizing rules to be somewhat tedious, but there's nothing I hate more than exceptions. So, in my first German course, I didn't complain about the three troublemakers (*"der"*, *"die"* and *"das"*) nearly as much as my neighbor Paola constantly did. She was one of those flamboyant people who find linguistic exceptions "charming" but the memorization of rules "uncivilized." That's why her German motto was, *"Der die das, des der des, dem der dem, den die das, aaaaaaaaaaarrrggggghhhhhhhhhh!"*

Herr Hartmut's teaching style made learning German exciting, but things could also get a little tense at times. One evening, for example, Paola made a mistake. She wanted to apologize, but only made the situation worse by saying the grammatically incorrect, *"Entschuldigung, Sie!"* (Excuse me, you!) This created a vicious cycle, as Herr Hartmut became ever more annoyed. He didn't allow any ifs, ands, or buts when it came to making mistakes. He repeatedly explained, "Young lady, it is EITHER *'Entschuldigen Sie'* (Excuse me) or *'Entschuldigung'* (Excuse me)!" Paola, however, didn't comprehend this and repeated exasperatedly, *"Entschuldigung, Sie!"* This little exercise pretty much took up the entire second half of the class that evening…

Most of us successfully completed the entire four-week course. For several of the students, this was due primarily to their having paid the tuition upfront. But not for me: I really enjoyed the course! And I was proud to be the only participant who didn't miss a single class. If I didn't succeed in anything else, at least I excelled in attendance.

During the course, we also learned a great deal about major German companies. For example, even though the shoe manufacturers "Adidas" and "Puma" are very popular in the U.S., it isn't widely known that these companies have German roots. The origin of the two companies' brand names is even less well known. The founder of Adidas was Adolf Dassler. Since his nickname was "Adi", he decided to shorten his last name and incorporate it into the brand name, thereby creating Adidas. After an argument many years later, his brother Rudolf left the company and founded his own, which he then named Puma. Fortunately, his name was not Derek-Dietrich, otherwise he might just have come up with a much less successful name for his new company, "Derdiedas".

On the last day of the course, Herr Hartmut informed us about the different tests you could pass in order to prove that you had learned some German. I stayed loyal to Herr Hartmut and took more courses. At the end of 1994, I passed the *"Zertifikat Deutsch als Fremdsprache"* (Certification of German as a Foreign Language) and a year later the *"Zentrale Mittelstufenprüfung"* (Intermediate Level Test). The Goethe-Institut offered other tests, but they were too difficult for me at the time. The innocent-sounding *"Kleines deutsches Sprachdiplom"* (Small German Language Certificate) was clearly over my head, and I didn't even want to contemplate the *"Großes deutsches Sprachdiplom"* (Large German Language Certificate).

After I passed the *"Zentrale Mittelstufenprüfung"* with a "very good", even Herr Hartmut's strict countenance softened a little. Beaming with pride, he said to me: *"Herr Bergmann, mit den Scheinen in der Tasche haben Sie jetzt den Beweis, dass Sie weder von Vorkennt-nissen völlig unvorbelastet noch von jeglicher Ahnung unbeleckt sind."* (Herr Bergmann, with these certificates under your belt, you now have proof that you neither have a complete lack of German knowledge nor are you completely devoid of any German language ability.) I stood there silently, but not because the scene was too sentimental for me, but rather because I could not remember if *"Vorkenntnis"* (previous knowledge) was masculine, feminine, or neutral. Aaaarrggghhhh…

P.S. At least German has the word "it" (*"es"*), just like English does. A language without an "it" seems suspicious to me. I stopped learning French immediately as soon as I found out that the language has no "it" at its disposal. For instance, in French, instead of saying "It rains", one has to say "He rains." Pardon me? Who is raining here?

5: We have Ways of making you talk … German!

When I began my German-learning-odyssey with Kerry's textbook, I thought that learning a foreign language pretty much consisted of just cramming vocabulary and grammar. After all, we didn't focus very much on a precise pronunciation in our highschool German class. Not until I had had some serious German learning at the Goethe Institute did I finally comprehend what one of the exchange students from Bonn had meant when she said that our highschool German teacher's spoken German was sometimes somewhat hard to understand. So when I received the command from Herr Hartmut to immerse myself in some cassettes and books on pronunciation, I complied without resistance. After all, I was getting fairly tired of always hearing comments along the lines of: "That sounded a little like German, but I couldn't understand a thing."

It may not be surprising that Arnold Schwarzenegger and I have little in common, but we do share one trait: We both have a relatively strong accent when we speak the other's native tongue. The ability to speak a foreign language without an accent is essentially based on three factors:

First of all, the age at which you begin learning the language is crucial. As many older language students note, with more than a bit of envy, children quickly learn how to speak a language without the faintest trace of an accent. But not even intellectual powerhouses such as Thomas Mann, Henry Kissinger, Albert Einstein, or Arnold Schwarzenegger were able to get rid of their thick German accents, even after they had lived in the U.S. for many years.

Secondly, experience with languages is very important: If you have already mastered one foreign language, then you are more perceptive to subtle linguistic differences in the next language you learn. This is comparable to playing a musical instrument. Generally, a middle-aged concert pianist could learn how to play the clarinet much faster than a person whose musical experience hitherto has been limited to turning the radio on and off.

Thirdly, natural ability plays a great role: Some have it, others don't. My brother Larry, for example, can imitate other people so well that they don't even get annoyed by his antics. I can't do this. Whenever I try to do impersonations, everyone within earshot gets irritated.

I first began learning German seriously when I was 22 years old. It was my first foreign language and I am not especially linguistically talented, hence the accent. From the beginning, I had expected to have difficulties in pronouncing the words with the umlauts, because these letters are obviously foreign. But I didn't suspect anything tricky with the rest of the "normal looking" letters of the alphabet. This turned out to be a major mistake. According to a book on phonetics, German has over 16 vowels and 3 diphthongs at its disposal, as well as 20 consonants. The syllabic structure is maximized in words like *"strolchst"* (you roam) and *"schluchzt"* (you sob) with at least three consonants at the beginning and four at the end. Furthermore, the book stated, "Pronunciation is the garment in which language encounters us as a form of oral communication". In this regard, I felt slightly underdressed.

It began with the first letter of the alphabet. In English, there is no difference between a short A and a long A. Up until then, I wasn't even aware that such a difference could exist. However, the German book explained in German that the short A is very short and the long A is very long. My ears took a long time to hear the difference between *"Stadt"* (city) and *"Staat"* (country), *"Fall"* (fall) and *"fahl"* (pale), and *"Wall"* (embankment) and *"Wahl"* (election). Regarding the pronunciation of the A in German, it seemed to me like it was *"die Qual der Wahl"* (the agony of choice).

A German proverb states *"wer A sagt, muss auch B sagen"* ("In for a penny, in for a pound", but literally: "Whoever says A must also say B.") In this case, whoever wants to say A correctly must also be able to pronounce E right. In English, German names like Christina and Christine are pronounced the same because we don't really differentiate between the pronunciation of an A and an E at the end of a word. (Both letters end up being the ubiquitous 'schwa' sound.) The people most annoyed by this phenomonon are German women with these names who live in America. But it also gets really annoying for Americans living in Germany when they try to ask their boss for more *"Kohle"* (cash) and he instead offers them a *"Cola"* (coke), since that is what it sounds like they requested.

***

I was beginning to fear I wouldn't be able to overcome all of these obstacles on my own. When I confessed this to Herr Hartmut, he referred me to the "department for difficult cases" where I would find professional help. A conscientious woman named Frau Güllicher was in charge there. I thought her last name was very appropriate: As soon as one was able to pronounce it correctly, one could claim to have reached one's linguistic goal. When I had my first meeting with her, she greeted me kindly and asked me a few questions in order to assess where my weaknesses lay. After a few minutes, she said, "Herr Bergmann, you need help. Maybe it's not too late." Somehow, this did not sound particularly encouraging.

During the first break, I went back to the coat rack – not to grab my coat and flee, but rather to hang up my pride right next to it. Frau Güllicher was a thorough and merciless teacher. My first assignment was to recite the alphabet. "What could be easier?" I thought, but her expression became progressively gloomier with every letter. Once I got to E, she couldn't take it any longer. "Wrong! All wrong!" Nobody had stopped me so early while reciting my ABCs since kindergarten.

Many Germans don't consider it to be all that bad if a foreigner's pronunciation is somewhat "imprecise", but when you mispronounce the word *"Bahn-Betriebskrankenkasse"* (health insurance for a railroad company) so that its abbreviation, *BBKK,* sounds more like *"Baby-Kacke"* (baby poop), then something simply needs to be done. My problem was that I pronounced the letters "in the English manner". In other words, less clearly and purely than in German and with more of a diphthong. For example, the English sound for O, like in the word "boat," is not pronounced as clearly and as long as the German sound for O in the corresponding word *"Boot"*. Also, the sound for E in English, like in the word "hey" is pronounced more like a German "ee-ii," in contrast to the German word *"Hee"* (eeee). (An example of which can be heard when listening to Klaus Meine of the Scorpions sing that he will "rock you like a huricaaaaaaaaaaaaaane".)

This tendency of English vowel sounds also influences the other letters because a German B is not just a B but also a *"Bee"* (the letter 'B'). Therefore, in German, there is no difference between *R* and *"Er"* (he), *T* and *"Tee"* (tea), *S* and *"Es"* (it), or *W* and *"Weh"* (pain). Many Germans enjoy using abbreviations in English such as "U R 2 hot 4 me" (you are too hot for me), without realizing they can do the same thing in German. For example, you could write, *"R trank T und S tat W"* (He drank tea and it hurt). However, Frau Güllicher was not amused when I asked her if a lowercase *'w'* could be called a *"Wehchen"* (a small hurt). When I saw the serious expression on her face,

I decided to act like the letter *M* or *"emsig"* (diligently).

Moreover, Frau Güllicher also explained to me that there are two other major differences between German and English pronunciation. One is that consonants are strongly aspirated in German. To point this out, she held a sheet of paper in front of my mouth and told me to say *"totes Papier"* (dead paper). When I did this, the paper was decidedly unimpressed. Then she held the sheet in front of her mouth and puffed out the same phrase. The sheet just about launched off. She then explained to me the third major difference, the so-called *"Knacklaut"* (glottal stop) in German, also known as the *"Stimmritzenverschlusslaut"* – which makes it sound more painful than it really is. This prevents individual sounds from being slurred together. This characteristic of German differs from French and English, where words are often combined in spoken language.

She summarized these three differences by changing the well-known saying to, *"Deutsche Sprache, deutliche Sprache"* (German language, clear-cut language). The crisp sound of German is the main reason why many non-German-speakers find the language harsh sounding at first. This characteristic is a double-edged sword for native English speakers: It simplifies listening comprehension, but renders one's own pronunciation more difficult. Native English speakers have a hard time pronouncing German because the muscles in their necks and around their mouths tend to need to be tensed somewhat more. On the other hand, it is generally easier for native German speakers to be understood when speaking English, as they are prone to speak overly clearly.

Frau Güllicher gave me many exercises in listening comprehension. In the beginning, I was unsure whether something was being paid in *"Raten"* (installments) or *"Ratten"* (rats), but I after a while could start to discern the difference. It was even more difficult to pronounce the *A* correctly. To practice this, I had to work through many ridiculous tongue-twisters, such as: *"Die Haare waren beharrlich, bis der Kamm kam."* (The hair was stubborn until the comb came) and *"Ich bin stadtstaatsalatsatt statt stadtsalatsatt."* (I am tired of city-state salad rather than tired of city salad).

I had fewer problems hearing the differences between the long and the short *E, I, O,* and *U* because they are similar in English, even if the sounds are spelled differently. This was then the main emphasis of the pronunciation exercises. The following are some unforgettable examples: *"Der Ofen ist offen, die Rosse fressen die Rosen, die Schotten essen die Schoten und die Motte ist in der Mode."* (The oven is open, the horses eat the roses, the Scotsmen eat the peapods, and moths are in fashion), and *"Der Pirat versucht, der Sucht zu entkommen, aber der Ruhm des Rums ist so groß, dass er bei der Flucht flucht"* (The pirate tries to overcome his addiction, but the fame of the rum is so great that he swears during his escape). Believe me, after a while the pirate wasn't the only one who was swearing...

When it came to the German diphthongs *AU, EI,* and *EU,* I just had to pronounce the vowels more tightly and quickly than in English. The umlauts, however, were a completely different story, which is why they have earned their very own chapter earlier on in this book. Among the consonants, the trickiest were *CH* and *R,* which is why they have also each merited their own chapters later on.

Danger was also lurking in every corner when it came to the German *L.* Contrary to the *CH* and *R,* I hadn't expected any problems with *L.* However, Frau Güllicher insisted that I was seriously mispronouncing it by forming the sound deep in the back of my throat. She explained it as follows: "When pronouncing the German L, your tongue should lie flat in your mouth like a petite princess in a waterbed. In English, however, the tongue lies like a sumo wrestler in a waterbed, causing the L sound to slide down the throat." The exercises for words beginning with an L were not so bad, but the words with an L following a vowel were rather painful – for Frau Güllicher. Before my private lessons with Frau Güllicher, I tried to avoid difficult to pronounce words like *"mehrere"* (several), *"griesgrämig"* (grumpy), and *"Nachrichten"* (news). Instead, I used their respective synonyms such as *"einige"*, *"quengelig"*, and *"Neuigkeiten"*. But there was no escape when it came to Frau Güllicher: I just had to fight my linguistic way through tons of terrible tongue twisters.

Thanks to Frau Güllicher's willingness to sacrifice and her high pain-threshold, my German listening comprehension and pro-nunciation skills improved over time. This was especially evident at my German *"Mittelstufenprüfung"* in December 1995, where only a few points were deducted for my pronunciation. I even received a compliment from a teacher who had flown over from Germany for this test: "Your pronunciation is not especially bad... for an American." Of course, this was similarly as flattering as "You don't play soccer that badly ... for an American." But at least it was a compliment!

Unexpectedly, I discovered a fringe-benefit of learning correct pronunciation. While learning how Germans speak German, I also realized how Germans speak English, which can be a useful thing in the USA. In Chicago, I knew a Swiss fellow named Gabriel who was pursuing his doctorate in engineering at Northwestern University. Gabriel was very popular in my circle of guy-friends, and not only because he was a likable chap, but also because he spoke English almost exactly like Arnold Schwarzenegger. Desperately, but in vain, Gabriel tried to rid himself of his accent, something which completely mystified us. I don't believe that he really appreciated our offering him money and other valuables in exchange for his reciting quotes from Arnold Schwarzenegger movies onto our answering machines. After my lessons with Frau Güllicher, I could imitate Gabriel (and thereby also Arnold) well enough that Gabriel liked me a little less.

Aptly for her career, Frau Güllicher only had a very slight German accent. But this is also the case for many of her fellow Germans. In a newspaper at the Goethe-Institut, I once read about German actors not being cast as Germans in English-speaking movies because they didn't sound "German enough". Unlike famous German-speakers such as Arnold Schwarzen-egger, Boris Becker, and Thomas Mann, these actors sounded to Americans like they had a somewhat shaky British accent. This, of course, unfortunately knocked them out of the running for acting roles as Germans. There was no danger of this happening to me. As Gabriel once said, "David, you are like one of these 'fake Amis' in the old movies who hardly make any mistakes but have a really strong accent!" I wasn't sure if I should take this as a compliment either...

P.S. In order to practice German pronunciation, Goethe's poem *"Heidenröslein"* was perfect for a *"Knäblein"* (little lad) like myself. Of course, Frau Güllicher was all too aware of this. After reciting the poem a multitude of times, however, an alternative version popped into my head. I called it *"Heidenarbeit"* (Found below, along with a very loose translation: "A little lad in the language lab").

"Heidenarbeit"

Sah 'ne Frau ein Knäblein steh'n,
Knäblein aus dem Sprachkurs.
Sprach so schlecht, es tat fast weh,
Lief sie schnell, es nah zu seh'n,
Sah's mit keinen Freuden.
Knäblein, Knäblein, Knäblein in Not,
Knäblein aus dem Sprachkurs.

Fräulein sprach: ich breche dich,
Knäblein aus dem Sprachkurs.
Knäblein sprach: ich grolle nicht,
Auch wenn du ewig quälst hier mich.
Denn ich will deutsch können!
Knäblein, Knäblein, Knäblein wird rot,
Knäblein aus dem Sprachkurs.

Und das strenge Fräulein half,
Knäblein aus dem Sprachkurs.
Knäblein sprach und sprach und sprach,
Bis es endlich sagen konnte .... "Sprach"!
Fräulein musst' nur viel leiden.
Knäblein, Knäblein, Knäblein ist froh,
Knäblein aus dem Sprachkurs.

"A little lad in the language lab"

Language lady saw a lad,
Little lad in the language lab.
Linguistically he lacked a lot,
She leapt to him and took a look,
Alas, her laughter soon went limp.
Little lad, little lad, little lad seemed lost,
Little lad in the language lab.

Lady lectured, "Here you'll not loaf,
Little lad in the language lab."
The lad spoke, "I'll not be lax,
However lengthy your lessons be,
Till my lips speak more 'Germanly'!"
Little lad, little lad, little lad labors long,
Little lad in the language lab.

And the lady lent a hand,
To the lustre-lacking little lad.
Laudably he listened and learned,
Until he lithely let loose a *"Sprach!"*
The lady listening less loathingly.
Little lad, little lad, little lad now can laugh,
Little lad in the language lab.

6: Sometimes the best Words come in small Packages

The German language has wonderful, almost indispensable "words", which aren't really words at all. At best, they could be called something like "wordlets". Despite that, these little wonders pack so much power that every language could actually be enriched by them. And, as such, they deserve to be especially appreciated. Here is a small selection:

Na

For a language that not only makes extremely long words possible, but also holds them in such high esteem, this little word can express a lot. It may only consist of two letters, but when combined with the right facial expression and appropriate tone of voice, this word can speak volumes. Even though one learns *"Guten Tag"* (Good day) in school, *"Na"* is the real German greeting. An exchange of *"Na?"* and *"Na?"* between two friends can pretty much serve as an entire conversation. Ultimately, the meaning of *"Na"* can range anywhere from "Great to see you again!" to "How are you?" to "Oh, it's you again." Moreover, a short *"Na, du"* ("Na", you) makes perfectly clear that you really like your conversation partner.

Boah

This sound is an explosion out of the throat resembling a cross between the sound made after a blow to the stomach and the sound of a meditating Tibetan monk. Children make it, for instance, when they hit their playmate directly on the head with a snowball. Men, on the other hand, use it when they see a Formula 1 race car go up in flames. And women emit this sound when they see that their favorite brand of shoes has been marked down 75%.

Hä

With this sound and the appropriate arching of the eyebrows and nose, you clearly inform your conversation partner that what he or she just said doesn't make the least bit of sense.

Tja

With this syllable, you don't even need distinct facial expressions or vocal intonations in order to express a countless number of reactions, such as: "You should have seen that coming," "I knew it!", "It's simply in the nature of things," "He deserved that," or "What was she thinking?" This little word's wide variety of meanings became the most obvious to me at my first dance class, when I messed up the Cha-Cha-Cha so badly that the dance instructor, shaking his head, renamed it as the *"Tja-Tja-Tja."* *Tja*, what can I say?

Pfui

Sometimes something is so bad that one can only say *"pfui"* to it. For example, in the theater when one suddenly realizes that one has spent a lot of money just to see a lousy performance, or when one's dog does something it definitely should not do. However, it should be noted that the comparative forms of *"pfui"* are not *"pfui, pfuier, pfuiest,"* but rather *"pfui Spinne"* (pfui spider) and *"pfui teufel"* (pfui devil). Alternatively, "Igitt!" is also an option.

Nanu

If you take the syllable *"na"*, and then tack the little word *"nu"* onto it, all of the sudden you have something brand new at your disposal: a word that quickly and cheerfully expresses that you are positively surprised.

Ach

Even though my father didn't speak Low German for decades, this sound was still often on his lips. After all, there is no comparable word in English that adequately expresses the same thing. All by itself, *"Ach"* can already convey a lot, but when it is combined with other little words, it comes into full bloom, as in *"Ach je!"* (Alas!), *"Ach was!"* (Yeah, right!), *"Ach nein!"* (Oh no!), *"Ach wirklich?"* (Oh really?), and "Ach so!" (I see!). Whenever I speak English, I have to take care that an *"Ach so!"* doesn't inadvertently slip out from my lips, thereby confusing all non-German-speaking conversation partners.

He

With these two letters, you get someone's attention. To hold his or her attention, however, you usually need a little more text.

Ne

With this sound one can say, "Or?", "Isn't that true?", "Or what?" or "I'm sure you see things the exact same way that I do!" Above and beyond that, one can use it to simply fill in the gaps in spoken sentences. Just as many French people cannot say anything without using the familiar French "uuhh" sound (pronounced somewhat similarly as in the English word "push"), many Northern Germans cannot end a sentence without uttering a *"ne"*. In Hamburg, a non-native-German-speaker's ability to convincingly employ the *"ne"* sound can almost enable him to pass himself off as a local. And when *"ne"* is combined with the word *"ja"* (yes), then something truly special is created. As my linguistically gifted Swedish friend

Camilla once said: "In no other language is there anything comparatively inviting and friendly!" *Ja, ne?*

***

This last "wordlet" reminds me time and time again of the first time I ever called someone on the telephone in Germany. This con-versation will always remain burned in my memory. It was in the late fall of 1994, and I was planning my first vacation to Germany in April of 1995. I intended to stay with distant relatives (Family E.). There was only one slight problem: my painfully limited vocabulary. And Family E. spoke, of course, only German.

I had my Great-Uncle Viktor to thank for my connection to Family E. He had contacted me in July 1994 for the first time. He said that the time had come to explain to me the birds and the bees of the Bergmann Family-Tree. Shortly before, he had learned from my father that I had minored in history at the university and then subsequently begun learning German. He took this as a sign of there perhaps still being some hope for my generation. As such, Great-Uncle Viktor declared that he was prepared to explain some things about our family history to me. Furthermore, he wanted to tell me about the connections between our homeland in Ohio and the area of Germany (between Bremen and Osnabrück) where most of our ancestors had come from. Strictly speaking, some of the German relatives could hardly be called "relatives", since the relationships were so distant, but Great Uncle Viktor said that one needn't be so strict when it came to family.

Coincidentally, about a month later, in August 1994, a large family reunion took place in my hometown. Viktor had helped to organize it, and even a few relatives from Germany were in attendance, including Herr and Frau E. After we had conversed with each other for a few hours using hand and foot motions along with my broken German, they actually invited me to visit them. Perhaps they did this out of pure politeness, because they had heard that in America people often invite "semi-strangers" over to visit them without actually meaning it. At any rate, I happily accepted their offer.

Several months later, I sat in my apartment in Chicago with a prepared text in front of me. I stared respectfully at the telephone. At this moment, I was no longer sure whether I was a man or a mouse. In the beginning, talking on the telephone in a foreign language was most difficult for me. Pedagogically speaking, a David (like many other humans) first learns reading comprehension, then writing, then listening comprehension, and subsequently speaking. Only much later does he dare to approach the terrible telephone. In short, whenever I make a call in a language I haven't yet mastered, the telephone lines are either *"besetzt"* (busy) – or they are *"besessen"* (possessed).

It took a great deal of willpower, but finally the man in me picked up the receiver and dialed the number. I prayed that *"Papa E."* would pick up the phone, because he awaited my call. Besides, his German was the least difficult for me to understand. The phone rang and someone picked up. But instead of the father, I heard a girl's voice. Nevertheless, I didn't panic. I asked – a little shakily -, "Is your father home?" After this tremendous accomplishment, I was confident that nothing could go wrong. She merely had to give one of the following answers: "Yes," "No," or "I don't know. I will ask my mother." But no, she gave me a five-word answer, of which I only understood one word, *"Ich guck mal eben, ne"* (loosely translated: I'm gonna getta look, *"ne"*). THEN came the panic. Luckily, shortly thereafter I heard the voice of Papa E., who kindly spoke slowly and clearly for my benefit.

In April 1995, I then flew to Germany and visited my distant relatives. Hospitable as Family E. is, they wanted to show me every sight near and far. So Papa E. suggested that I take part in the traditional May 1st bicycle tour, which usually lasted several hours. Since I hadn't been on a bicycle for a long time in the not very bike-friendly city of Chicago, this suggestion made me a little nervous. I thought to myself that all of that physical exertion must be the real reason why May 1st is called "Labor Day" in Germany. But to my relief, during the bicycle tour we spent much less time actually on our bicycles than in the beer gardens along the route.

Papa E. also suggested that I go on a *"Wattwanderung"* (hiking tour in the tidelands) with them. However, since I didn't know yet what the word *"Wattwanderung"* meant, I thought it might just be something in Low German, since they often spoke that dialect among themselves. Therefore, I thought my follow-up question would be more polite if I expressed it in Low German: *"Eine Wat-Wanderung? Wat is' dat?"* (Some what-wandering? What is that?) To be honest, every step I took during that vacation was some form of "what-wandering"….

During my visit, Mama E. was especially disappointed that she hadn't learned any English in school. She asked me the meaning of certain words in English and was surprised to discover how easy it could be. After all, some words are almost the same in both languages, such as *"Hand,"* *"Finger,"* and *"Arm."* The same is true for newer words like *"Telefon,"* *"Roboter,"* and *"Restaurant"*. Sitting together in the living room one day, however, she declared in German with a sigh something along the lines of: "David, you're lucky: English is everywhere today. Just look at the stereo system! Everything on it is in English." She summarized her opinion consisely with a High-German/Low German mixture of: *"Dat is' ganz schön fies, wat!"* (That is a nasty trick, what!) In this way, Frau E. learned a little English and I improved not only my standard German, but also my Low German on the side.

After surviving my first vacation in Germany and realizing how much German I had learned during my two weeks there, I was glad that Family E. hadn't spoken English with me. Even though I generally appreciate Germans being very hospitable, sometimes they get a little too enthusiastic with their hospitality around foreigners. As soon as they notice an accent, many switch right on over to English. Sometimes Germans switch even before they have heard my accent. For example, I experienced this years later after a Christmas Mass in Switzerland when I was introduced to the German priest. He immediately started talking to me in English about his time in the States. After a few minutes of this, I said something to my friend Bodo in German. The priest looked as if he had seen a miracle and cried out, *"Boah! Gott im Himmel! Sie sprechen Deutsch! Wieso haben Sie das nicht gleich gesagt?"* (Heavens above, you speak German! Why didn't you say so right away?) I had to confess: He hadn't asked me, and one is generally reluctant to interrupt a priest.

Even though I understand that Germans mean well, sometimes it can get a little bothersome when they unexpectedly switch over to English on me. To avoid misunderstandings, I once came up with a little parable: "Once upon a time, there was a little German. Although he liked his native country very much, he considered Denmark to be just wonderful. This passion prompted him to study Danish for years and to save his money. Then one day he quit his job and moved to Denmark. There he tried to get to know the country and to master the enchanting Danish language. However, in every conversation the well-meaning, yet unknowing Danes told him the same thing, 'Little German, it may be cute that you are trying to speak our language, but let us speak German instead, as this must surely be easier for you.' His eyes full of tears of disappointment and frustration, the little German gives up and moves back home."

As the author of this parable, I thought its lesson was clear enough. I believed it could solve my dilemma of allowing me to speak German with Germans without insulting them. However, the quintessence of the parable proved to be a too little opaque for many of them. Some were curious why anyone would want to learn Danish when English is so much more practical. Others asked themselves if the little German comes from Flensburg. And others wanted to speak Danish with me afterwards. All this was not exactly what the author had had in mind.

Ach nein?

7: We would like some "Fahrvergnügen", please.

My new German teacher in Chicago, otherwise extremely patient, was almost at his wit's end. As much as he tried to drill it into me, I just could not remember the new German vocabulary word he was trying to teach me: *"Vergnügen"* (pleasure). Then, suddenly, it dawned upon him: "You know, David, the word is just like *"Fahrvergnügen"* (driving pleasure), only without the '*Fahr*!" In a flash, the word was burned into my memory.

One of the most unforgettable TV commercials of the 80's was the one from Volkswagen which introduced the German word *"Fahrvergnügen"* to the unsuspecting American public. This word made quite an impression on us: A small, stylish Volkswagen zipped through the American landscape to the tune of a cheery German song playing in the background. A German song on American television was already something exotic, but the sound of that word *"Fahrvergnügen"* was even more so.

"Fahrvergnügen" is only one of many snazzy German words that have found their way into the English vocabulary over the centuries. Others include *"Realpolitik"*, *"Hintergrund"*, *"Poltergeist"*, *"Schaden-freude"*, *"Kindergarten"*, *"Zeitgeist"*, *"Angst"*, *"Wanderlust"*, *"kaputt"*, and *"Meister"*. As the editor of a major American newspaper once wrote, "Those Germans seem to have a word for everything!"

Nevertheless, the origin of these words is often unknown to Americans. One time, for instance, after I had sneezed, my mother asked me, "David, by the way, how do you say 'Gesundheit!' in German?" I couldn't really blame her for this, since it was not until after living many years in Germany that I finally realized that the omnipresent word "Delicatessen" is also of German origin. Or that the "Spritzer" which you can buy there also comes from German.

Especially ironic are the "Doppelgänger" (another German word often used in English) which show up whenever English and German simply exchange each other's words. For example, the game which the Germans refer to as *"Kicker"* is called "foosball" (pronounced similarly to the German word for soccer: *"Fussball"*) in the USA. What we Americans refer to as "backpacks", more and more Germans now like to call *"Bodybags"*, whereas in Great Britain they are actually refered to by their German name *"rucksacks"*. And whereas Germans get a kick out of calling the men in the American soccer team *"die US-Boys"*, in America, the "Über-Basketballspieler" Dirk Nowitzki is called a "German wunderkind".

Once, while one of my clients was driving me to the train station in Cologne, we listened to the CD of the new musical *"Tanz der Vampire"* (Dance of the Vampires) along the way. (By the way, this was the first musical written originally in German.) At a particularly lovely part of the musical, he said to me, *"Herr Bergmann, das ist das sogenannte 'main theme' des Musicals"*. ("Mr. Bergmann, that is the so-called 'main theme' of the musical.") Evidently, my reply took him somewhat by surprise: "That's very ironic! In English, that is what we would call a 'Leitmotiv'!"

On account of the size of German immigration to the United States over the centuries, large numbers of Americans have German last names such as I do. However, many Americans don't know what these names actually mean. I realized this when, together with friends, I was watching the American quarterback Frank Reich during a football game. In American football, there is a defense manoeuvre called the "Blitzkrieg" (or "Blitz" for short). When the commentator said, "The defense leveled Frank Reich with a blitz!" I just had to laugh. I was the only one in the room. (Evidently no one else realized that *"Frankreich"* is the German word for France: the last big country to go down under a real-life German blitzkrieg.)

A further example came during an American baseball game in the early 90's. The pitcher was Los Angeles' Jim Gott (the German word for "God") facing at bat San Diego's second baseman Tim Teufel (the German word for "devil"). Most Americans were unaware that they were thereby witnessing what truly could be considered the very oldest rivalry in the entire world of sports.

I found the unintentional humor of the sport commentators in this situation to be "über-funny". As in German, in English there is no comparative form for the word "super". Something is either super or it isn't; there is no "superer". In order to fill in this gap, the English language has borrowed the German word *"über"*. For example, when the word "Supermodel" is inadequate to express a woman's beauty, she is called an "Über-model", even if she isn't of German origin like the famous lovely ladies Claudia Schiffer, Heidi Klum or Nadja Auermann.

Should I ever get employed by the American marketing departments of VW, BMW, or Mercedes Benz, I would definitely recommend that the new advertising slogan somehow include the words "Über-Fahrvergnügen" and "Übermodel." Americans would definitely find the products simply irresistible!

***

By the way, my new, patient "Über-German-Teacher's" name was Alexander. Even though he was "the Great" to me, he didn't actually come from Macedonia, but rather from the vicinity of Kassel. And, instead of Asia Minor, he had been conquering the American continent ever since his early youth.

Even though it was indeed very effective, over time learning German at the Goethe-Institut became a little too expensive for me. As a result, I resolved to search for some less costly knowledge. After the last lesson in the Goethe-Institut before a long summer-break in 1995, I discovered a flyer from a German student named Alexander on the bulletin-board. In order to partially finance his expensive studies in Chicago, he was offering private German lessons.

That evening I rang his number on the phone: An American voice answered the telephone. Confused, I asked if a German by the name of Alexander lived there. In English he answered: "I am the German by the name of Alexander." Astonished, I replied: "Seriously?" while thinking to myself, "Why doesn't he have a German accent? Is he trying to pull my leg or what?" Alexander answered: "I know what you are thinking: Why doesn't he have a German accent? Is he trying to pull my leg or what?" I mentally nodded my head and was genuinely impressed. Then he started talking to me in German. Not only did he want to thereby prove his German identity, but he also wanted to see how sure-footed I was with the language. For the first time, I didn't think it was so bad that I have an accent in German. Nevertheless, I still think it would be nice to be able to turn it off in emergencies, for example before a language exam.

Alexander and I met up once a week in various bars, where we discussed a wide variety of topics in German. I was greatly impressed by everything Alexander was doing in Chicago: a dissertation, various freelance projects, diverse translations, and many women. I asked him where he found the time for all of this. He explained that when one does so much simultaneously, one either must do it all either "*zack, zack*" (loosely translated:

zoom, zoom) or *"ruck, zuck."* (very loosely translated: zippy zappy)

I learned many important things from Alexander which I would otherwise never have found out about at the Goethe-Institut: for example, what German women want. He told me that German women are generally more independent and less sentimental than American women. They know what they want and, in particular, they don't want any *"Weicheier"* (softies) or *"Warmduscher"* (wimps). Alexander noted that he would probably have to put in some overtime hours with me when I said, "But I like *"weiche Eier"* (soft eggs) and *"warme Duschen"* (warm showers). Fortunately, he didn't ask me if I had a *"weiche Birne"* (was soft in the head), due to my slight mistakes which caused such big differences in meaning...

Disappointed by his pitying look, I tried to prove to Alexander that I was also cool, so I said casually, *"Die Kellnerin hier ist ganz schön knusprig."* (The waitress here is really crispy.) Alexander knew what I had meant to say and therefore said, "David, you should keep your American accent at all costs. When you make mistakes like this, German women will still forgive you for them, maybe even the *"knackige"* (firm and toned) ones." His expertise really impressed me. And it got even better yet. He explained further, "David, girls can fall for the right accents: When I was new in Chicago and still had a German accent, a few female students took German lessons from me just because they thought my accent was hot. Some even wanted to give me a tip of oh so much more than 15% – they wanted to head to bed with me..." I had never thought about such a concept before. Yes, to me, Alexander was truly "the Great".

During one lesson, Alexander also explained "The Secret of the Lucky Pennies." At that time in Chicago, you still had to pay for a one-way subway ticket with small silver-colored tokens costing $1.50 each. After learning at the Goethe-Institut about the popular German concept of the *"Tageskarte"* (day-pass) for subways, I was disappointed that there wasn't such a thing in Chicago. My disappointment quickly faded, however, when Alexander showed me that the Chicago subway-tokens were the exact same size as German pennies.

During my next vacation in Germany, I went into a small-town bank in order to get myself thousands of German pennies. The employee asked me curiously why I needed so many coins. In my thick American accent I declared: "In Chicago, these pennies are very valuable for certain transactions." I thereby probably helped to perpetuate the myth of Al Capone and Co. in that bank. Unfortunately, this mafia-like-method only worked up until 1998, when the highly-efficient Chicago bureaucracy was tipped off by a very subtle hint: millions of German pennies circulating in the subway vending-machines.

I couldn't thank Alexander enough for his valuable tips. In the process, I discovered many ways to express gratitude in German. This definitely doesn't go hand-in-hand with the stereotype of Germans being an ungrateful people – something which the Germans themselves actually seem to believe. Thanks to a popular American song from the early 60's, almost every native English speaker knows the expression *"Danke schön"* (thank you very much), even though few can pronounce it correctly. Although they may not enjoy the same world-wide renown, the alternatives in German are numerous: *"Danke sehr", "Ich habe zu danken", "Danke vielmals", "besten Dank", "herzlichen Dank", "tausend Dank", "recht schönen Dank", "Ich danke dir", "Ich bin dir dankbar", "Ich möchte mich bei dir bedanken", "mit tiefer Dankbarkeit", "ein herzliches Dankeschön"*, and of course, *"Danke"*. And, as if these many choices weren't already enough, Germans seem to enjoy borrowing corresponding expressions from other languages, such as: *"Merci"* (French), *"Grazie"* (Italian), *"tusen takk"* (Danish), and *"muchas gracias"* (Spanish). Exceptionally enough, in this case, the Germans seem to prefer NOT using an English expression, perhaps because "Thank you" just doesn't seem to roll smoothly off of German lips.

Now and then I was able to make Alexander laugh so hard that I started asking myself who should really be paying whom here. For instance, he once asked if I was familiar with *"Die Sendung mit der Maus"* (The Show with the Mouse – a popular German children's TV Program featuring a seriously smart mouse as the main character). When I answered with certainty: "Of course! That is the German expression for 'E-mail'," he wasn't able to stop laughing for the rest of the afternoon. (I had not yet learned that the German noun *"Sendung"* doesn't only mean the verb "to send" but also the noun "show"...)

One weekend, I showed Alexander my office at the CPA firm where I worked in Chicago. It was located in one of the smaller skyscrapers (on the 42nd floor). Up there we had a spectacular view of the city skyline. However, like in most skyscrapers, the windows could not be opened. After all, sticking one's head out too far at such a height is the best way to lose one's head... Or, as the Germans like to put it so eloquently by combining two common idioms into one new longer one: *"Wenn man sich zu weit aus dem Fenster lehnt, ist man schnell weg vom Fenster."* (If one leans too far out of the window, then one is apt to soon disappear from the scene entirely.)

In my opinion, the library was the best place in the entire office, and not just because of the books, but also because it had such large windows. Looking out through them, we were astonished to find that the window seemed to look back at us! On the other side, two slightly unkempt window-washers were at work, wobbling on their platform. They didn't seem to have noticed us and continued on with their job. When I saw how high up the men were from the street, I was reminded again why I had become an accountant: It's considerably less frightening than being a skyscraper-window-washer!

Although he at times seemed almost immortal to me, Alexander evidently had a fear of heights. He asked me how I could work on the 42nd floor every day. When I explained that a person gets used to it, he gave me a skeptical look. Then I asked him how he could have endured living for decades in Kassel, only a few kilometers away from the concentrated military might of the Soviet army. I should have seen his answer coming from a long way off: "Well, you get used to it."

Afterwards, as we zoomed "*ratzfatz*" with the elevator downwards, Alexander seemed to enjoy an inordinate amount of *"Fahrvergnügen."*

8: Future (-tense) Shock

As mentioned earlier in this book, forming the past-tense in German can be rough for the poor proverbial Chinese guy, but forming the future-tense could be right up his alley. In contrast to many other European languages, which usually use a future form, in German the customary procedure is simply to take the present form along with an expression of the time. Even Germans who speak English without an accent therefore give themselves away when they say something in English along the lines of: "I give you the book later." (This would be the direct translation of the grammatically correct German sentence: *"Ich gebe dir das Buch später."*)

In German the word *"werden"*, can be used for all sorts of things, for instance for the creation of the so-called *"Futur I"*. I made myself somewhat unpopular during the early phase of my time in Germany when I still thought that I needed to use the word *"werden"* (in the sense of "will" or "shall") in order to express a certain future. When I heard a polite request from a fellow student somewhere along the lines of: *"David, gibst du mir einen Stift?"*, I translated this directly as: "David, Are you giving me a pencil?" I therefore responded: *"Im Augenblick schreibe ich mit einem Stift, aber ich **werde** Dir einen geben, wenn du einen haben möchtest."* (At the moment, I am writing with a pencil, but I will give you one, if you would like to have it.) Clearly, this is not the best way to endear oneself to the native student body...

In German there is a whole range of possibilities when it comes to expressing the fact that one is going to do something in the near future. And each one has a slightly different shade of meaning. As such, it took me quite a while to discern the nuances of meaning when given the various answers to my often posed question: "When do we want to go to lunch?".

The answers spanned a whole spectrum of words such as *"demnächst"* (in the near future), *"bald"* (soon), *"gleich"* (immediately), *"sofort"* (at once), *"sogleich"* (instantly) or *"jetzt"* (now). Many complete sentences were also difficult to decipher, such as *"machen wir umgehend"* (we'll do it right away), *"unmittelbar nachdem ich meinen Kram erledigt habe"* (immediately after I have gotten my stuff done) or *"wir gehen gerade."* (we are already on the way.)

In the early phase of my stay in Germany, I asked politely what precisely the difference among all of these expressions could be. The responses which I received were partly helpful, but then again only partly:

- „Sage ich dir gleich."
- „Das hängt davon ab, ob die Person, die es sagt, ein Mann oder eine Frau ist."
- „Nun, nun!"
- „Verschwinden Sie auf der Stelle!"

And here the translations:

- I'll tell you straight away.
- It depends on whether the person using the phrase is a man or a woman.
- Now, now!
- Get out of here on the spot!

It seemed to me that I would need to be basically clairvoyant in order to clearly see all of the various shades of meaning. Therefore, usually my follow-up sentence was not another question, but rather a simple demand: *"Nenne mir eine Uhrzeit!"* (Give me an exact time!)

***

In the summer of 1995, I pondered on how my future should look. One thing was absolutely clear: I could not take it any longer in my little one-room apartment in Chicago – it was simply too cramped in there. As such, the other residents and I had a vote to decide which of us had to move out. In spite of my running a vigorous election campaign, most of the cockroaches voted against me... So I had to hit the road.

Shortly thereafter, I moved to a northern suburb into an apartment inhabited by two women. Coincidentally, both had a connection to the German language. One was named Alexis who was studying opera singing. There may not be many professions in the USA for which a good knowledge of several foreign languages is a huge advantage, but opera singer is definitely one of them. Alexis only knew a few phrases in various languages, but she did not let this discourage herself in her "diva-ishness". She explained to me somewhat haughtily: "I may not speak much German, however, I do have an excellent pronunciation!" I was not completely convinced, as she tended to "mis-correct" me again and again.

On my second day in the apartment I got a little shock once I came home from work. Upon entering the apartment I heard what sounded like screaming coming from the shower. I thought to myself: If we are lucky, the hot water has run out. If we are unlucky, we are under attack. I should perhaps mention that, at that time, I was not yet familiar with Alexis' musical-scale singing exercises...

The other flatmate's name was Sabine. Both of her parents originally came from Europe. Her mother fled as a small child with her parents from Latvia at the end of World War II, whereas her father fled years later from East Germany shortly before the Wall was erected. Sabine's grandparents were all very proud of her facility with languages, however, they were correspondingly disappointed that she had studied Spanish instead of Latvian or German. I could hardly imagine how it must be, not to be able to communicate fluently with one's very own grandparents. (My Grandma may have spoken Low-German, but she also spoke English as a second native language.) Sabine's grandmother, on the other hand, lived in a suburb of Leipzig, Germany, and did not speak a word of English.

Even though her name did not appear on the rental agreement, an additional flatemate lived in the apartment: Alexis' cat, which had been clairvoyantly named "Pandora". Although she was a rather clever cat, Pandora seemed to have great difficulties distinguishing between my backpack and a kitty-litter-box. This character-flaw of hers set my writing career back by years.

In the apartment below us lived Joon, a Korean. At the age of eight, he immigrated with his parents to the USA. Although he had never returned to Korea, he still possessed a Korean passport. When I asked him once why he never had gone back for a visit, he responded: "My parents only spoke a form of "children's-Korean" with me, I have not had any Korean friends here, and I have never watched Korean TV. As a result, for the past eighteen years I have spoken the language like an eight-year-old." Joon was also afraid that, should he ever set foot on Korean soil, he would be immediately drafted into the army. His language limitation made such a prospect even less appealing to him. He explained that, should an army officer yell at him, he could only give a reply along the lines of: "I no understand. Please no owies for me." I asked Joon whether he had any interest in learning Korean. He answered: "I prefer learning Japanese and German. Those are the cool languages." As I said, Joon was a decent fellow.

Back in those days, I usually did my homework in the library. Libraries are fine places, especially in the USA, where the opening hours are much longer, for instance on Sundays and evenings until 9:00 p.m. On one particular Sunday in April 1996, I found the library in my suburb of Chicago to be even more splendid: In the lobby I clearly spied two pairs of German spectacles – two pairs of female German spectacles!

To my astonishment, I gradually realized over the years that I could recognize Germans in Chicago, even if Germans tend to reflexively copy many fashion developments from the USA. Fortunately, there are still a few exceptions. For example, spectacles are a completely different matter: Here the Germans are often way ahead of the Americans. As such, I could identify the two German girls already from a distance. I snuck closer and my first impression was confirmed, as I heard them speaking German. I gathered my courage and addressed them as follows: *"Ich werde nächste Woche in den Urlaub nach Deutschland fliegen."* (I will fly to Germany next week for vacation.) I was prepared for all sorts of responses from them, but not for the one that I got: *"Schön für dich."* (Good for you.)

But I did not give up. Fortunately, the two of them were even more confused by the catalogue-referencing-system of the American suburban library than they were by my sudden appearance in their midst. I recognized my opportunity and made them an offer: I would show them the library and initiate them into the mysteries of its usage, if they would promise me not to immediately run away from me. The two of them looked at each other, then at me, then the library. This process was repeated several times until they finally said: "O.k." And thus I met Anja and Nicole.

Both had just recently arrived in the USA as Aupair- girls. After a tour of the library, I noticed that they were pleased to finally have met a young American who not only knew where Germany was located, but also was aware that its inhabitants also had modern conveniences aplenty there such as cars, refrigerators and TV's. Most of all, they were impressed that I, as an American, even knew that Bonn was Germany's *"Hauptdorf"* (capital-village).

We made a deal: I would chauffeur them around Chicago in my car, and, as compensation, they would spend time with me. What a bargain! Best of all in their opinion, was my being able to speak some German, and thereby being able to help them out with some of the more tricky aspects of American English.

The first "interrogation" took place that very evening in a nearby pub. Anja and Nicole wanted to know how to translate practical German words into English which they could not find in any standard dictionaries. Examples included such words as: *"Streber"* (geek), *"Spießer"* (nerd), *"Klugscheißer"* (wise-ass) along with various other expressions which I would rather not repeat here…

Many of their inquiries were indeed too much for my *"Wörterbuch"* (often referred to by them as my "German Dictionary", whereas I called it "The Book of Knowledge"). After several failed attempts in finding a particular translation, Anja lost her patience and renamed my little buddy as *"Scheißding"* (crap-thing). Fortunately, in spite of all of this we could be of assistance to one another: They simply needed to describe the slang term in question and I then had to let my imagination run wild in order to come up with a suitable translation. Sometimes it felt to me like we were playing some sort of Pictionary.

The experiences of the past months had only strengthened my resolve to really and truly learn the language of my ancestors, so I resolved to live for a time in Germany. But, as the proverb says in both languages, the devil is hiding in the details. I considered how to best go about it. Would I be able to find an office job in Germany? Probably not, since who would hire a "work-permit-less" foreigner like me? Should I become an Au-Pair-Boy? No, I already felt too old to be bossed around by kids. Should I become what the Germans called a *"brotloser Künstler"* (a penniless artist, but literally a "breadless artist")? No, I had already heard too many rumors about how good German bread tastes. Should I become an old student? Hmmm … why not actually?

I discussed this idea with many people. Some were impressed, whereas others scoffed at the mere concept. My parents, however, were brought to the very verge of tears. Not primarily because they would miss me, but rather because they didn't want to even think about who might have to pay off my new mountain of student loans. They didn't know yet that studying at a university in Germany is considered to be a basic human right, with the result that it is almost free of charge. Even for non-taxpaying, free-loading foreigners like me!

Fortunately, Anja supported me in this endeavor, not only with the various applications and translations, but also with the deliberations on which German university would suit me the best. First of all, Anja needed to spend a few hours just convincing me that German universities are all more or less created equally. After all, in the USA there are huge differences in quality among the universities. For admission to some of them, all one needs are two things: an adequate amount of money and a pulse. At other universities, in contrast, geniuses with perfect grade point averages are rejected if they cannot demonstrate sufficient extra-curricular prowess, for instance: Olympic medals, a contribution to the reduction of the regional crime rates, or the discovery of a cure for a widespread disease. As a result, the college diplomas in the USA vary greatly in terms of prestige and worth.

Taking all of this into consideration, I applied to several German universities. And some of them even admitted me! But only the *Universität Göttingen* informed me of this in a timely manner, in other words, BEFORE the beginning of the semester. As such, my decision was clear: Göttingen. Not merely because of the good reputation, the central location and the plethora of beautiful old buildings, but also because they processed my application *"unmittelbar"* (immediately).

9: To "ihr" is Human

For native English speakers, conjugating German verbs is somewhat complicated. Even "regular" German verbs require a good deal of effort, for instance the run-of-the-mill word *"reden"* (to talk): I *"rede"*, you *"redest"*, he *"redet"*, we *"reden"*, you all *"redet"* and they *"reden"*. Of course, as the very name of their category implies, the "irregular" verbs are even trickier, for example the word *"sprechen"* (to speak): I *"spreche"*, you *"sprichst"*, he *"spricht"*, we *"sprechen"*, you all *"sprecht"* and they *"sprechen"*. When it comes to verb conjugation in English, on the other hand, a simple, solitary S gets into the action, and then only rarely: I "speak", you "speak", he "speaks", we "speak", you "speak", they "speak".

English may have, similarly to German, numerous irregular verbs, but only a single one of them is troublesome in the present-tense, "to be", in other words: I "am", you "are", he "is", we "are", you "are", they "are". While learning German, I was actually very grateful for the stubborn little English verb "to be", as it made conjugating German verbs much easier for me to master. When confronted with a new German irregular verb, I simply asked myself what "to be" would do in such a situation.

When it comes to German verbs, the easiest thing is the so-called *"Siezen"*, which is addressing someone using the formal form of "you". In this respect, the German verbs are all well-behaved. On the other hand, the so-called *"ihrzen"* (addressing a "plural you") can be much harder. In itself, *"Ihrzen"* is not any more grammatically complicated than *"duzen"* (the familiar form of "you"), one just doesn't hear it nearly as often. A non-native German speaker is, for example, simply not used to having the umlauts disappear from certain verbs, as in the sentences *"Ihr **lauft** zu langsam"* (you all run too slowly) or *"**Fahrt** ihr mit dem Taxi?"* (are you all taking a taxi?).

This is why I tried out all sorts of tricks in the beginning in order to avoid having to do any *"ihrzen"*. Unfortunately, this tended to backfire on me. Once I even tried a non-existent *"du-alle-Form"* (as in the English "you all"), but this was only understood by German-speaking Americans from the South, but not by actual Germans themselves. My solution back then was to use the formal *"Sie"* form on every group. (This is easier because the *"Sie"* form is the same in the plural as in the singular.) This eventually landed me in a small town high-school in the middle of Germany. Allow me to explain…

***

One day in March 1996, I was on my way in Chicago to a music store. At a stoplight, I found myself suddenly surrounded by a group of German high-school girls out on a field trip. As I would do a few months later in the library with Anja und Nicole, I spoke to one of them in German with my thick American accent. All of the sudden, a hush settled over the entire group.

Once they had recovered from their shock, they became curious, and we got into a conversation. My using the formal *"Sie"* form when addressing them caused several of the girls to giggle. They told me repeatedly that we did not need to be so formal, but I responded as amiably as I could that I simply was not capable of using the *"ihr"* form, as my German was not good enough. Fortunately, my various linguistic weaknesses were not bad enough to prevent them from giving me their telephone numbers when we parted. I don't believe that I have, before or since, ever received so many women's telephone numbers at one time! They invited me to visit them in Germany should I, by chance, one day be in the neighborhood of Fulda.

„One day" arrived only two months later, as I was then on my second vacation in Germany – and I found myself, in fact, just around the corner from Fulda. Since I had just recently decided to study in Germany, I wanted to take a look at several of the universities before I sent off my applications. After visiting Göttingen, I took a slight detour to Fulda. Once there, the girls clearly wanted to bring me to their high-school in order to show off "their real American" at an impromptu session of "Show and Tell".

One of the teachers was especially interested in my story and asked me all sorts of questions during the class. One of his first questions was: *"Herr Bergmann, haben Sie Familie?"* (Mr. Bergmann, do you have a family?) My answer: *"Ja, ich habe eine Mutter, einen Vater und drei Brüder"* (Yes, I have a mother, a father and three brothers) may have been factually correct, but the intent of his question had been to find out whether I had any children of my own. Once again, I was surrounded by the now very familiar sounds of German teenagers giggling.

After the first hour, "my" girls told me: "David, you should really meet ‚Adelheid von B.'." Adelheid had namely spent a year in England and could therefore speak English better than anyone else. When we met during the lunch break, we first spoke German. After a few minutes the conversation turned to birthdays and ages. Adelheid revealed to me that she was a *"Jungfrau"*, which means "virgin" in German. She then asked me what I was. I thought to myself: Alexander was right! German women sure are very direct! I answered therefore, "I don't have a girlfriend, but I am not telling you whether I am a virgin. That is too personal." She had to reflect a while upon my rather odd answer, but then she seemed satisfied with my response. (Only later did I learn that *"Jungfrau"* also means "Virgo"…) She then continued the conversation in English in order to avoid any similar misunderstandings.

My stay in Fulda only lasted a few days, but subsequently Adelheid and I stayed in contact by writing letters back and forth. She also supported me in my decision regarding which university to attend. I appreciated her help, even if I gradually began to get the impression that she was not acting entirely altruistically. She graciously offered to pick me up at the airport, in the event that I would study at the *Universität Göttingen*. To top it off, she even offered to let me stay with her family until I had found my own place.

It thus came to pass that in August 1996 I was picked up at the Frankfurt airport by a real life noble-woman. It felt to me like royal treatment. I could hardly believe it, but there at the station stood a *"Freifrau"* (Baroness), who was smiling at me. Adelheid's father was a *"Freiherr"* (Baron), and, as such, she was a *"Freifrau"*. She had to explain this to me several times before I believed her and before I completely comprehended the implications, but then I was duly impressed. In English, not only don't we have any thing along the lines of *"der, die, das"*, but we also don't have any *"von, van, de, di, da"* and so on. Officially, we don't even have any nobility whatsoever in the USA. In my hometown, there are quite a few people with the last names of *Herzog* (duke), *Koenig* (king) and *Kaiser* (emperor), but apart from their noble-sounding names, these people don't have anything else resembling blue-bloodedness.

During my history classes in the USA, we had learned about all sorts of important people who had sported a *"von"* in their names: glorified men such as Johann Wolfgang von Goethe, Helmuth von Moltke, Friedrich von Schiller and Otto von Bismarck. And when I studied the First World War more closely, I learned that General Ludendorff needed to have Paul von Hindenburg at his side at the head of the German Imperial Army, since he himself did not possess a "von" in his name. Adelheid explained to me, however, that those days when the "vons" ran things in Germany were basically over. She even claimed that the only advantage of being a real "von" consisted of being allowed to officially shorten the *"von"* to a *"v."*. Compared to this *"Freifrau* von Importance", I felt like a country boy, with the designation of "David *Unschuld vom Lande, frei von jeder Ahnung"* (David, Bumpkin of the Country, Free of any Inkling).

The family had four children, and Adelheid was the oldest at age 19. Her mother had spent a year in England a while back, so she was decidedly Anglophile. For her it must have been a welcome diversion having a young American man in the house as a guest. She found me to be kind of charming, even if I did sometimes amuse the family with my rather odd antics.

While staying at their home I picked up more valuable bits of cultural information, for instance:
- Cold weather means putting on a pullover inside, not putting the heater up to maximum.
- Shoes are to be worn outdoors, the indoors are reserved for *Birkenstocks.*
- Leaving the lights on in empty rooms can cause all sorts of "burnouts".
- Knowledge regarding "The Backstreet Boys" is crucial in impressing the girls.

One of Adelheid younger sisters was especially pleased to have an American in the house. At least until she realized that I knew much less about The Backstreet Boys than she did. At first she did want to believe my declaration of ignorance and instead insisted that I should "Stop playing games with her heart", as the "BS-Boys" used to sing. It was the fall of 1996, and The Backstreet Boys were at the peak of their popularity in Germany. No wonder, I thought, once I realized that their main competition consisted of a long-haired Irish family living on a boat (The Kelly Family). At that time in the USA, the "BS-Boys" were basically unknown. Although they originally came from Florida, they did not become a hit in the States until a few years later. By that time, I was fully prepared to impress the American girls with my profound knowledge of Backstreet Boys basics.

Adelheid's mother found some of my little mistakes adorable. For instance, I misunderstood the instructions at a crosswalk and hugged Adelheid until we were allowed to cross the street. After all, the sign said: *"Drücken und auf Grün warten."* (Squeeze and wait for green. – Little did I know that the word *drücken* also meant "press" – as in press a button.) Or when I related how nice it was when Adelheid hugged me for the very first time. (I used the word *"umgearmt"* instead of *"umarmt"*, which sounds to a German less like hugging and more like wrapping tentacles around someone.)

Unfortunately, Adelheid found some of my mistakes slightly less amusing. Once, when I wanted to ask her if she was very cold, I translated my query directly from English into: *"Bist du noch sehr kalt?"* (This sounds to a German more like "Are you still a frigid woman?") Instead of an answer, she just gave me the cold shoulder...

I quickly realized that entering a McDonald's was absolutely out of the question for Adelheid. In fact, she couldn't even bring herself to use the restaurant's real name, but, similarly to many Germans, rather used all sorts of nicknames, such as *"McDoof"* (McDumb), *"McDreck"* (McDump) or *"Schmecktdochnichts"* (tastes like nothing). One evening, as I was on a little excursion with her and a friend of hers named Christoph, I suggested this. She replied resolutely: "No! I never to go a *„McDoof"*! I never give money to American capitalists!" Suddenly she realized with whom she was talking, and then continued somewhat abashedly: "… except for David."

A few hours later, Adelheid was suddenly much less brash. She didn't feel well, and definitely needed some sweet sustenance. Her only hope was a glass of orange juice at the "Restaurant with the Golden Seagull", as Christoph called it. With a deep sigh, she realized this as well. Then, just as Caesar stood before his Rubicon, Adelheid found herself shaking in front of the entrance to the burger shop. Christoph and I had to wait outside; she did not want anyone to witness her sweet defeat. Contrary to her own expectations, Adelheid emerged unscathed from within after a short period. As a prank, I pretended to see some ketchup at the corner of her mouth. Measured by the ferocity of the strong language which she then unleashed upon us, we were fairly certain that, recharged with orange juice, Adelheid was once again at full strength.

I quickly learned two further linguistic rules from Adelheid regarding women. First of all: when a woman asks a man how she looks in German, he should never answer: *"Ganz gut"*, even if it literally means "entirely good", since its connotation for some unknown reason is "not that bad". Secondly: When a woman asks a man whether she is too chubby, he should never answer: *"Es geht."*, as this sounds too much like "eh". (In this manner, a Bergmann can quickly become a "bogeyman" …)

Compared with her mother, Adelheid's father wasn't at all sure what to make of me. This was partly due to his not speaking English very well, as he had never lived in an English-speaking country. As a result, he had considerably more difficulties understanding me. When he told me that my German was *"einzigartig"*, I was pleased, at least until the younger sister explained to me the difference between *"einzigartig"* (unique) and *"einzigartig gut"* (uniquely good). At least I could take some comfort in having left the stages *"abartig"* (strange) and *"eigenartig"* (peculiar) behind me…

The only thing about me that shined in his eyes was the golden ring on my right hand. When Adelheid's father glimpsed it, hope sprang up in his heart that perhaps his daughter had indeed fallen for a man of high rank. He asked me whether I had inherited the ring from my father and whether he also owned huge tracts of land. I truthfully responded that my father had a few acres which he farmed, but that after he had helped to finance my university studies he was now by no means a man of means. (I had bought the ring myself shortly before my graduation from college as a sort of immodest memento.)

I could see the disappointment in the good Baron's countenance. In an attempt to console him, I explained that my university in the USA is one of the elite institutions of higher learning. When he asked for the its name, I replied: "Notre Dame du Lac" (the university was founded in the 19th century by a French priest). Full of élan, Adelheid's father exclaimed: *"Ah bon! Vous parlez français?"* My confused expression quickly told him that, in this area, I possessed neither "Savoir-faire" nor "Know-how". For him this meant only one thing: yet another disappointment!

Later on, Adelheid's father showed me his *"Meisterschein"* in carpentry. (This is a certification as a master craftsman). When I asked why he needed such a thing, it was certainly not my intention to insult his pride. Back then I simply was not aware that the concept of carpentry in Germany is a lot different than in the USA, where anyone can do basically anything with his own property as long as no one is physically injured in the process.

It was becoming clear to both of us that I did not have any hidden skills. I realized, moreover, that without hidden skills I was a poor choice in his eyes. But at least I had to use the formal *"Sie"* form when addressing the Baron. One weekend Adelheid invited me to accompany her to the theater. During the performance of an older piece by Schiller I realized to my horror that in the olden days in Germany, the polite form of you was not *"Sie"* but rather *"ihr"*. If I had had to use my stumbling comprehension of the *"ihr"* form with Adelheid's father, there is no telling how low I could have sunk in his esteem...

At least Adelheid's father could take some comfort in my living in Göttingen, which was about an hour distant from his daughter. As such, at least I could not constantly exert a negative influence on her. Adelheid was less thrilled by this arrangement. I tried to console her with the fact that we could at least telephone daily with each other. She looked appalled and simply said: "David, *von wegen!*" (David, no way!)

Evidently, not even a Baroness could afford to indulge in such extravagant behavior.

10: Idiosyncratic Idioms

As a curious child, I once wanted – for whatever reason – to know just how many islands there are exactly in the Pacific Ocean. To my disappointment, I realized after a long search that I could not find a concrete figure anywhere. None of the reference works let themselves be pinned down on the matter to an exact number. Most of them just gave estimates between so-and-so many thousands. But I did not give up until I finally found an explanation in one of them. Even if scientists – thanks to new technologies – now have a much better grasp of the huge ocean, an exact number of the Pacific islands will never be determinable since the ocean never remains static. While some islands pop up above the water's surface, others are being submerged. Besides, it is even open to debate where exactly to draw the line between a real island and a simple rock with a bit of dirt strewn on it. I shrugged and decided to stick this factoid into my mental desk-drawer marked "Things I will never know".

In some ways, the number of idioms in a modern language is similar to the number of the islands in the Pacific. In fact, perhaps it is even more extreme. Very few of them are rock solid, known by just about everyone, and seemingly predestined for eternity. Others are only known in small circles or disappear almost as fast as they once had appeared.

Often I hear Germans complaining about the large numbers of idioms in the English language, apparently without realizing that there are at least as many in German. Some experts even claim that, of all the languages in the world, perhaps none has more than the German language.

In contrast to native German speakers, German learners notice fairly quickly that the language is practically overflowing with idioms. However, sometimes their meanings aren't always evident at first glance. As such, lots of diligence is required. After all, the Germans don't say the following for no good reason: *"Knapp daneben ist auch vorbei!"* (Slightly to the side is also off-target.) Ironically, in the beginning I was slightly off-base with this idiom as I used to say: *"Knapp daneben und dann ist vorbei."* (Slightly off-target and then it is game over.)

After I had already lived in Germany for several years, a friend of mine named Tom gave me a big, fat book about German idioms as a birthday present. Although the book enabled me to improve my German skills, the language thereby lost a bit of its colorfulness in my eyes. For example in the case of these idioms:

"Ich freue mich wie ein Schneekönig."
(Literally: I'm happy as a snow-king.)
When I first saw this idiom, I immediately imagined a man who looked somewhat like Santa Claus's brother. He wears a crown on his head, has a herd of snowmen in his service and is simply satisfied with his existence as the lord of the snow. In the book, however, I learned that the word *"Schneekönig"* is simply an additional term for the bird called *"Zaunkönig"*, which stays in Germany during the winter and sings a cheerful song.

"Das macht den Kohl nicht fett."
(Literally: That doesn't make Kohl fat.)
As probably lots of other people before me had done, the first time I heard this idiom I immediately thought about Helmut Kohl. Even though the former German Chancellor seemed seldom to turn down any food, this idiom seemed to imply that not even he ate everything placed in front of him. In the book, however, I discovered that the saying instead referred to the fact that a juicy piece of meat can make a portion of

cabbage ("*Kohl*" in German) taste much better. (Upon learning this, I found the mental image of such a chubby "Chancelor Cabbage" funny in its own right…)

"*Die Frau hat Haare auf den Zähnen.*"
(Literally: The lady has hair on her teeth.)
Upon hearing this idiom for the first time, I thought that perhaps the lady had hair on her teeth because she had eaten some soup with hair in it. Naturally this would darken her mood. The book, however, pointed out that the idiom derives from the belief that hairiness is a sign of manly strength and courage. Should a woman have hair on her teeth, then she is considered to be so very manly as to be abrasive and aggressive.

"*Das ist ein heißes Pflaster.*" (Literally: That is a hot bandage.)
This idiom caused me to think of a man with a fresh flesh-wound which needs to be treated by a doctor with a bandage. The last thing that the man would like to see in this situation is a steaming hot bandage being placed upon the wound. In the book, however, I discovered that the word "*Pflaster*" also means "pavement", so that a "*heißes Pflaster*" can be a dangerous part of town where one can easily be injured.

"*Jemanden aus der Bahn werfen.*"
(Literally: To throw someone out of the train.)
When I first encountered this idiom, I pictured a man thrashing wildly about as he is being thrown from a speeding train, either because he didn't have a ticket or because he had really annoyed the conductor. The book explained, however, that this saying means that someone has simply been unexpectedly thrown off-track by an event. (The word "*Bahn*" not only means "train", but also "track".)

"Es ist noch kein Meister vom Himmel gefallen."
(Literally: No master has ever fallen from Heaven.)
Upon hearing this idiom, I thought that only apprentices fall down from Heaven, as the masters surely know how to stay up there in Paradise. The book informed me, however, that this saying means that one first has to learn and practice something before they become competent at it.

"Die Hosen anhaben." (Literally: To have the pants on.)
This idiom caused me to imagine two people locked in combat, of which only one is wearing pants. The other must have dropped his drawers previously. Since the pants-less-person is much more preoccupied with his half-naked existence, the pants-wearing person clearly has the upper-hand, just as the armored knight does in a duel with a lightly armed peasant. In the book, however, I learned that this saying stems from the time when pants were an article of clothing worn only by men back when they ruled the household. (Soon thereafter, I realized that we actually have the same expression in English which made my misunderstanding all the more embarrassing…)

"Die Katze im Sack kaufen." (Literally: To buy a cat in the bag.)
Here I was certain that one naturally would like to see the cat beforehand to ensure that it is a "top-of-the-line feline". The book stated, however, that one has no interest whatsoever in buying a cat. The reference to a cat stems from the days when a worthless cat was placed into the bag instead of a yummy rabbit in order to trick a careless buyer.

"Das geht auf keine Kuhhaut." (Literally: That goes on no cowhide.)
The source of this idiom was a particular mystery to me. A few

possible explanations popped into my head: Maybe it is hard to write on cowhide? Perhaps it was a holy cow? Maybe the cow resisted out of principle? However, the book pointed out that this saying stemmed from a medieval belief that the Devil recorded all of the sins of a dying man onto a piece of parchment made of cowhide. I see.

Normally it is not a catastrophe when one slightly garbles an idiom, but exceptions prove the rule, as I learned during my search for an apartment in the city of Göttingen …

***

In my opinion, I was fully equipped: I had a fully-loaded telephone card, a city map, and I had meticulously planned out what I needed to say. I dialed the telephone number. A woman's voice answered, stating her last name. As confidently as I possibly could, I declared: *"Guten Tag! Ich habe gelesen, Sie vermieten ein vermöbeltes Zimmer."* ("Good day! I've read that you are renting out a **trashed** room.") Only much later did I learn that instead of saying *"vermöbelt"*, I should have said *"möbliert"* (furnished). And already our con-versation was at an end. One thing that I evidently did not yet have at my disposal was a clue.

It is seldom easy finding an abode in a new city. It is even more difficult when this city is located in a foreign country – especially one where the language is still in many respects a stranger. So there I stood, somewhat at a loss, in a telephone booth in Göttingen, where I intended to study. In fact, it had not been all that long ago that I didn't even know that there was such a city named Göttingen – a state of knowledge which many Americans maintain throughout their entire lives.

A few weeks prior, in July 1996, I had quit my job in Chicago. My colleagues asked me curiously where my new job would be. After all, surely no one would leave their place of employment without a new position at a better company securely in the bag. I explained to them: "I have been accepted to a German university in a city by the name of Göttingen." All around me were quizzical looks. "It is nearby to Hannover." The facial expressions of those around me became not only more confused, but now also rather skeptical. I continued: "It is between Hamburg and Munich." Then they all exclaimed (even in German – more or less): "Ahhhh, Munich! *Guten Tag!*" Yes, sir, that there is a city named "Munich" in Germany where the natives say *"Guten Tag"* to one another on a daily basis is common knowledge in the USA.

After my first telephone conversation in Göttingen it was clear to me that I would have to quickly get up to speed with the local lingo and customs if I wanted to find a home in this homely city full of old buildings. There are days when one learns more than otherwise in an entire month. My first day in Göttingen was such a day. Fortunately I was not alone. At my side was my best friend on German soil: my dictionary.

With him clutched tightly in my hand, I had looked over the numerous apartment offers in the cafeteria on the university campus at the break of dawn. Unfortunately, many of the bits of information were shrouded in mystery to me. As such, in my eyes the bulletin board was more of a "blackbox". I was trapped in a jungle of abbreviations, and not even my little quadratic buddy could help me out: *WaMa, BaWa, FB, VB, NB, WB, BZB, ETW, ETG, CT, KT, ZH, RH, DH* etc. Furthermore, I was unsure what the difference could be between *Etage, Stock, Geschoss* and *Stockwerk* – after all, my little buddy translated them all into English as "floor". At least I found it plausible that a *"Warmmiete"* (warm rent) cost more than a *"Kaltmiete"* (cold rent), even if I was not exactly sure what the temperature related details entailed…

After a while of standing in front of the bulletin board, I had jotted down several telephone numbers. Armed with these, I marched resolutely to the telephone booth. In order to gather some courage, I recalled just how much German I had learned over the past two and a half years. On the other hand, I was well aware of the fact that here in Göttingen, not only I would have to converse with complete strangers, I would have to ask complicated questions. What was even worse, I would have to understand complicated answers!

In the telephone booth, I paid my dues in the form of several ten- mark-telephone cards. After awhile, I myself began to feel similarly devalued. Fortunately, the whole business was not in vain after all. An elderly lady by the name of Frau Wilbärt realized that she had found in me a real treasure. A treasure to be plundered, that is! After all, I clearly was a completely defenseless potential tenant.

At the end of our conversation, she asked me: "Herr Bergmann, where is your telephone booth?" Fortunately, not even my slightly mangled response could scare her off: "It is a 'cat's throw' in distance from the new Town Hall." She simply replied: "Stay where you are. I will pick you up right away!" (Only later I was to learn that in German one can say either *"Katzensprung"* (a cat's jump) or *"Steinwurf"* (a stone's throw), but talking about *"Katzenwurf"* will just land you in trouble with the animal loving populace of the country...)

Shortly thereafter, she drove me to her house which stood on a small hill. Once at her door I hesitated briefly, for a sign caught my attention: *"Vorsicht! Bissiger Hund!"* (Caution! Dangerous Dog!) I asked Frau Wilbärt where this hard-hearted hound was hanging out. She answered: "There is no dog here. Every house has such a sign. It is just a matter of course." I considered this to be strange enough, but a second sign worried me even more: *"Bitte die Füße abtreten!"* (literally "Please hack your feet off!", but actually "Please wipe off your shoes!") I thought to myself: "How brutal!"

Hanging on the wall in the stairwell was a funny photo of a colorfully costumed Frau Wilbärt. Once she saw my inquisitive countenance, she explained: "Herr Bergmann, that is a photo from '*Fastnacht*'." Thereupon she asked me whether I knew when this *"Fastnacht"* took place. I answered jovially: "But, of course!", and thought to myself that *"Fastnacht"* probably occurred between *"Spätabend"* (late evening) and *"Nacht"* (night). What I couldn't figure out, however, was why people dressed up in such silly outfits before going to bed... (*"Fastnacht"* is actually Mardi Gras, and NOT, as I first mistakenly deduced "almost night".)

While climbing the stairs, Frau Wilbärt mentioned that the room was on the top floor. Once there, I realized upon seeing the furnished "broom-closet-sized-abode" that in this building the top floor and a "top-apartment" were not necessarily the same thing.

In order to conceal my disappointment, I tried to think of something nice to say about the little mini-room. But my comment that the room looked like a *"stilles Örtchen"* (literally: "a place of solitude", but more commonly understood as a euphonism for "a toilette") did not seem to comfort Frau Wilbärt at all. She explained to me that once a week a cleaning lady from Ghana would stop by to clean the room. In answer to my question, how much extra that would cost, Frau Wilbärt answered: "The cleaning is already included in the rent. It is not all that expensive since the woman does *"Schwarzarbeit"* (black-market work)." While I pondered whether *"Schwarzarbeit"* had anything to do with the "dark continent", Frau Wilbärt continued in a whisper: "But you shouldn't tell anyone about the '*Schwarzarbeit*', otherwise it is 'lights out' for us." I tried to nod my head understandingly.

After this long day, I no longer was very picky. The walls in the room were slanted, but otherwise nothing seemed to be seriously askew. And after all, the room didn't have to be perfect. My wallet just told me that it had to be perfectly cheap. I therefore sealed the deal with Frau Wilbärt by signing my name on the dotted line of her rental contract. I was very pleased to have found my new abode. Even if it wasn't actually *"vermöbelt"* (thrashed).

11: Textbook-German vs. Colloquial-German

Lying on the table in the "broom-closet-kitchen" were several napkins. Apparently, Frau Wilbärt had "borrowed" these from an Italian restaurant, for on each one were the translations of many common Italian phrases into German. While snacking during a television commercial, these inspired me to create my own linguistic napkins. On left side of these would be the German found in textbooks, and on the right side the German found almost everywhere else: The kind which livens up everyday conversations. This German is referred to by non-scientists (to be honest, as of yet actually only by me) as *"Budendeutsch"*. Here the very first edition of the *"Dudendeutsch-Budendeutsch-Serviette"* (Textbook-German & Colloquial-German Napkin):

Ja & Jaja – („Yes" & "Yes, yes")
Once *"ja"* is good. Twice *"ja"* can either be twice as good or only half as good: It depends on whether the tone of voice rises or falls. When it rises, it means: *"Oh, ja!"* But when it falls, *"jaja"* actually means something more along the lines of: *"Mache ich. Mag ich aber nicht."* (I'll do it, but that doesn't mean that I like it.)

Nein & Nee – („No" & "Nah")
During my second vacation in Germany I snapped up the word *"Nee"*. Back in Chicago I met up with Anja in order to show off my improved German language skills in a conversation with her. Every so often I casually tossed a *"Nee"* into the conversation. With an admonishing finger, Anja said to me in German: "David, you shouldn't use that word." To which I replied: "But, Anja, you use it all of the time!" *"Nee*, I

never do." We both had to chuckle at that. She had never noticed that she said *"Nee"* at least as often as she said *"Nein"* until an American showed up to point it out to her.

Keineswegs & Nö – („Under no circumstances" & "Uh-uh")
"Keineswegs", like *"keinesfalls",* is a wonderful word which is unfortunately simply too long for certain situations. Then the succinct little word *"nö"* just fits better. Even though it is very short, the word *"nö"* not only has the same meaning as *"keineswegs",* but it also has several additional connotations such as: "What were you thinking?" "How did you get that impression?" along with "Don't even think about trying to change my mind!"

Selbstverständlich & Na logo – („Of course" & "Yuh-huh")
Similarly to the word *"keineswegs",* the word *"selbstverständlich"* is a wonderful, yet perhaps somewhat lengthy word. If one would like to succinctly, yet nonchalantly, express one's agreement with the aforementioned statement, then all one need do is let loose a *"na logo".*

Entschuldigung & Vorsicht! – („Excuse me" & "Look out!")
In my German class, I learned that when one must disturb someone else in order to get through, then one should say, *"Entschuldigung",* just as we say "Excuse me" in English. It seems, however, that in everyday German the expression *"Vorsicht!"* is much more common. With this word, one makes clear that his or her forward progress is somehow the problem of others. It is similar with the polite words *"Verzeihung"* (pardon) and *"Pardon"* (pardon – but with a French accent), which can be replaced by *"Mach Platz!"* (make way!) and "Darf ich einmal durch?" (May I pass by?)

Frohgelaunt & Gut drauf – („Joyful" & "Doing fine")
Like the words *"frohgemut"*, *"frohsinnig"* and *"froh"*, the word *"frohgelaunt"* is, without a doubt, a great word. However, nowadays it no longer seems to be always in fashion. Whenever one wants to demonstrate his good spirits, then one declares that one is *"gut drauf"*. Even better yet: *"super gut drauf!"*

Herausragend & Turbogeil – („Superb" & "Turbo-wicked")
If the German words *"hervorragend"* (excellent), *"herausragend"* (superb), *"ausgezeichnet"* (outstanding), *"wunderbar"* (wonderful) or *"großartig"* (great) just aren't good enough, then one just needs to avail oneself of any of the words containing the word-stem: *"geil"* (literally: horny). Examples include: *"affengeil"*, *"oberaffengeil"* *"oberaffentittengeil"* or *"turbogeil"*. Though these literally translate as "monkey-horny", "super-monkey-horny", "super-tits-monkey-horny" and "turbo-horny", they all actually mean "great". Inexplicably, my favorite word thus far in this connection, *"topgeil"* (how Tom Cruise looks in a cool fighter jet), has thus far not yet been able to achieve general acceptance. (In this regard I must make a confession: The first time that a woman told me after she had accomplished something cool: *"Ich bin so geil"*, I slightly mis-understood her meaning, to the disappointment of all parties involved. (How was I supposed to know that it had two meanings, its literal translation of *"I'm so horny"* along with its more figurative meaning of "I'm so awesome"?)

Nicht wahr? & Oder was? – („Isn't it?" & "Or what?!")
For many situations, the expression *"nicht wahr"* is simply too timid. The same holds true for the friendly southern German *"gell"* and the northern German *"ne"*. In contrast, a resolute *"Oder was?"* convey a certain conviction and sounds almost like a challenge: *Oder was?!?!*

The main source for my new napkin of knowledge was a massive portion of TV-German. Allow me to explain: In order to remain in my new abode in Göttingen, it was not enough for me to merely pay my rent on time, I needed a residency permit. In order to land one of these permit-prizes, it didn't suffice to just find the right person at the foreigners' office, I needed to be admitted to the university. And to arrange this, I needed not only to pay the tuition fees, but also to pass a test, more specifically a language proficiency examination. Indeed, if I wanted to get anywhere at all, I would need to prove that I understood more German than just the word "*Bahnhof*" (train station). And time was short, for after I had moved in to my new broom-closet, only a little more than a week remained left to me before the admissions-test at the beginning of September.

Unexpectedly enough, my savior turned out to be the one and only Frau Wilbärt. Soon after handing me the keys to the apartment, she unwittingly handed me my key to success. "Herr Bergmann, so that you, as an American, feel more at home, I have dug the TV remote-control out from down in the basement." She snickered "Heeheeheehee", as she glimpsed the twinkle in my eyes. She misunderstood, however, the true basis for my joy: At that moment I realized namely that I was now optimally equipped. My grammar knowledge, reading comprehension, and writing skills in German were already passable, but I still had some major room for improvement in the areas of listening comprehension and vocabulary. As soon as the sounds of her giggling had faded away down the stairwell, my TV-studies could commence in earnest!

I found this to be a relative stress-free way of learning: I just sat on the chair, watched, and gathered in knowledge. During my lessons in Chicago I had already learned that there are various dialects of German, but I soon noted that there are also various dialects of TV-German, of which some were easier to understand than others. In the beginning, I found the commercials the best, since the sentences were short and succinct, the images were flowery and fluid, and these seemed to complement each other wonderfully for my comprehension. But the best thing about the commercials was the repetition, the repetition, and the repetition …

The German soap operas were also perfectly suited for my needs. By the end of the week, I was well-versed in the details of *"Gute Zeiten, schlechte Zeiten"*, ("Good Times, Bad Times") *"Verbotene Liebe"* ("Forbidden Love") and *"Jeder mit jedem"* ("Everyone with Everyone"). Though, to be honest, I am no longer certain if the last one was really called that… By then I had noticed that I could understand the grandmas and grandpas in Germany much better than the teenagers, since the senior-citizens normally spoke more slowly, clearly and correctly than the "wild youngsters". But in these soap operas I could easily catch the young actors' and actresses' sentences, since they were so short — and besides, in-between there were always so many come-hither glances.

The German news reports, on the other hand, were much too complicated for me. The sentences were too long and the vocabulary words too hard. Even more demanding than the news, however, were "The Simpsons". For the first time ever, I realized just how quickly they spoke. Until then, the beloved, yellow cartoon-family had always managed to make me laugh, but now the tears in my eyes were no longer those of joy. It is often claimed that one has mastered a foreign language when one dreams in that language. I would venture to dispute that assertion. But when one completely understands every sentence in a foreign language version of the Simpsons, then there is no longer any doubt: That language has indeed been mastered.

After several days of intensive TV-studies I felt a bit like the Karate Kid when he tried to catch flies using chop-sticks – the new vocabulary words seemed to just flutter elusively about my head. Then a solution occurred to me: if I held the remote control in my left hand, then I could write down words which recurred often with my right hand and look them up later in my "Book of Wisdom". These I could then add to my Deutsch-English-Vocabulary lists which I memorized while I was on the go. Ah: repetition, repetition, repetition.

During the first week of my TV-studies, there were all sorts of surprises in store for me. For instance, I discovered that German scientists had evidently cloned the American Late-Night comedian David Letterman. This comedy-clone seemed to have just about everything from Mr. Letterman: similar jokes, similar stage, similar format, etc. Only his name sounded German: Harald Schmidt. Although I by no means understood all of what he said, after a while I had to admit that Herr Schmidt had some funny original jokes.

Watching him reminded me of my first encounter with the German dubbing of American movies and TV-shows: The actor Billy Crystal was a guest on David Letterman's show in the early 1990s, as he wanted to do some publicity for his new movie. As a joke, Letterman had decided to show excerpts from the German dubbed version. The audience was highly entertained. Back then I also laughed, but in the meantime I was no longer amused. Until then, many American viewers were not even aware that there were dubbed versions of American TV-shows being shown in foreign countries. Billy Crystal complained about the characteristics of "his" German voice, which, in his opinion, just didn't sound right. I could now sympathize with his feelings: I had similar misgivings about the sound of my voice in German.

The next big surprise was one of the biggest actors from the

German-speaking world: Arnold Schwarzenegger. I was really excited when I saw the opening scenes. Arnold is extremely popular and beloved among American men. Not only on account of his huge muscles, but also because of his pronunciation, which is as tough and cool as he himself is. Finally, I now had the chance to enjoy his real voice! But then my excitement turned to disappointment: Even though the movie was in German, Arnold did not have his own voice, but rather had been dubbed by a stranger! I found this hugely disappointing, but also slightly understandable. (And probably more understandable than his real Austrian accent in German would have actually been for me ...)

I looked for something better and, flipping through the channels, stumbled upon the movie "Four Weddings and a Funeral" with Hugh Grant. Unfortunately, this, of course, was also dubbed into German. I quickly realized after a few minutes that Hugh Grant without his English voice is about as helpless as Superman with a hunk of Kryptonite in his hand. This waste of his thespian talent seemed about as sensible to me as if his beautiful then-girlfriend, Liz Hurley, would be working at a radio station.

In Germany, one could almost get the impression that not only Arnold and Hugh, but also Eddie Murphy, Sean Connery, Bruce Willis and all other "Stars of the Hollywood-Heavens" speak perfect German. Fortunately for my TV-studies self-confidence, the voices just did not fit perfectly with the lip-movements, no matter how well the dubbing had been done. This does not seem to bother most Germans, probably because they have grown up with it. For me, however, it was a difficult adjustment. After all, the few foreign-language films shown in the USA are usually shown with subtitles. The most noteworthy exceptions were the Kung-Fu- and Godzilla-Films of the 1970s. These really confused my schoolmates and me back then. And not only because the lip-movements didn't fit with the voices, but also on account of Godzilla's somewhat unusual strategy of monster-world-domination. Why he kept attacking Tokyo while all of the other gigantic evil creatures had New York in their sights was simply inexplicable to us.

Without a doubt, the biggest surprise for me during my TV-studies was the discovery of one of my favorite TV-shows from my childhood: "Hogan's Heroes" (In Germany: *"Ein Käfig voller Helden"* or literally "A Cage full of Heros"). I had not expected to find this show on German television for several reasons: The show is older than I am, the quality is at best questionable, and the plot revolves solely around how witty Allied soldiers outfoxed dumb Germans in World War II. I would have thought that the Germans would have been about as receptive to such a show as the French are about encountering the London subway-station "Waterloo" upon arriving in England.

Be that as it may, I was pleased as punch. As is the case with many American men, most of first jewels of my German vocabulary came from just this TV-show: *"Raus, raus, raus!"*, *"Eins, zwei, drei"*, *"Nein"*, *"Jawohl, Herr Kommandant!"*, *"Fräulein"*, *"Hofbräuhaus"*, *"Mmmm … Strudel!"* and *"Dummkopf"*. We kids loved using these very practical expressions at home – and they gave me a tiny head-start for my subsequent German learning, so to speak a *"Vorsprung durch TV"* (Literally: "Head start through TV."

As a raider of the lost vocabulary words, I was thrilled with my TV-studies. My prey was everywhere. In the Chicago of the mid-1990's, this was definitely not the case. There it was nearly impossible to get a German TV-education. At most, back then one could buy a satellite dish and then pay lots of money to receive *"Deutsche Welle"*. And this station was not even completely in German! In contrast to the French equivalent, TV5, the "Deutsche Welle" transmitted lots of shows which informed people about Germany in various languages. I suspect that TV5 would rather rename itself to "Waterloo TV" than broadcast in languages other than French.

Hm, I wonder how you would say *"Nö!"* in French…

12: Reflecting on German Reflective-Verb

In the German language, verbs are not only reflected more often than in English, but also in a wider variety of ways. Of course, this can have serious consequences for anyone learning the language. For instance, when I told Anja in German in the summer of 1996 that I was planning to "change my clothes" in the autumn (*mich umziehen*), she gave me such a funny look, that I considered moving away immediately. (I should instead have said *"umziehen"*, which means "to move one's place of residence". Not until she asked me whether it wouldn't be a better idea to change my clothes everyday did I realize my mistake…)

Other mistakes regarding the reflective verbs may sound slightly wrong to German ears, but they are not strange enough to cause a native speaker to correct a German learner. It therefore took me a long time until I figured out that I was making mistakes by saying the following: *"Ich wasche meine Hände"* (I am washing my hands.) or *"Ich putze meine Zähne und kämme mein Haar"* (I am brushing my teeth and combing my hair.) Correct German would be *"Ich wasche **mir** die Hände"* and *"Ich putze **mir** die Zähne und kämme **mir** die Haare."*

In English we rarely have to use the reflective verbs, though there are cases of this, such as in sentences like: "He is enjoying himself." Normally we only use them in order to emphasize something, as in the sentence: "I bought MYSELF a hat or "I am shaving MYSELF" In fact, in contrast to German, we could just leave the reflective part off without confusing people.

In German there are three different categories of reflective verbs. First of all, the verbs which are not usable without their reflective pronoun *"sich"*, such as *"sich schämen"* (to be embarrassed), *"sich beschweren"* (to complain) and *"sich benehmen"* (to behave). Secondly, there are the verbs which can be used reflectively or not, as is the case with many English verbs. Thirdly, there are the verbs which have a different meaning depending upon whether they are used reflectively.

This third variety is especially difficult for German-learners, as these sentences demonstrate:

- *Sie **verspricht** ihm, **sich** während ihrer Rede nicht zu **versprechen**.* (She **promised** him not to **misspeak** during her speech.)
- *Er **nimmt an**, dass sie **sich** der Aufgabe **annehmen** wird.* (He **assumes**, that she will **accept** the assignment.)
- *Sollte er **sich** auf dem Weg **verlaufen**, wird der ganze Tag schlecht **verlaufen**.* (If he **gets lost** along the way, the whole day will **go** badly.)

A native English speaker can easily picture the following expressions: *"man bewegt sich"* (one moves oneself), *"man verletzt sich"* (one hurts oneself) or *"man setzt sich"* (one sets oneself down). After all, these expressions are very figurative. It gets more difficult to visualize wordings such as *"man entscheidet sich"* (one decides) or *"man freut sich"* (one is pleased), since we don't use reflexive verbs in those situations. ("One decides oneself" sounds odd enough, but "one pleases oneself" could be especially embarrassingly misunderstood…)

Of course, sometimes some funny misunderstandings can arise in German when a native English speaker has not yet mastered the fine art of German verb reflecting. One time, for example, when Adelheid and I returned from hiking, her mother said that, before we had supper, *"wir uns lieber duschen und umziehen sollten"*. Since Adelheid was well acquainted with the English language, she understood immediately what my broad smile and slight blush meant that I was thinking. As such, she replied: *"Auch wenn meine Mutter sagt: ,Ihr solltet **euch*** *duschen', meint sie nicht zusammen!"* (Even though my mother said: "You should shower yourselves", she did not mean together!") She continued, that I should not only shower by myself, but also cold. Her facial expression also indicated that the same also was valid for phrase *"sich umziehen"* (change clothes)...

***

Since it is well known that man cannot live alone on air and learning, during my first weekend in the broom-closet apartment I took off for a little shopping tour. Along the way, I thought to myself: "Ah, there is nothing better than a little shopping tour on a lovely Sunday morning." That is what I thought...

I remembered having seen a big sign in the store-front window of a neighborhood supermarket the day before during the trip in Frau Wilbärt's car. In big, bold letters were written the words: *"Durchgehend geöffnet!"* (Open continuously!) To me, the message of the sign was crystal clear: Here I can shop 24 hours a day, 7 days a week! But as soon as I caught sight of the store from a distance, I got an uneasy feeling in my stomach. Germans may like to say *"Morgenstund' hat Gold im Mund"* (literally: "The morning hour has gold in its mouth"), but this early hour just left a bad taste in my mouth. I took a close look at the sign and then looked through the window-pane of the store. The supermarket was deathly still. Since not a single soul was in sight, I quickly realized that I didn't even have the option of haggling.

My exploratory walk continued through the surrounding area. I passed by many lovely, attractive stores. Lots of lovely, attractive, closed stores. The rumbling in my stomach just got louder. After a while I finally gave up on my quest. When I returned home, hungry and disillusioned, I saw Frau Wilbärt working in her garden. I asked her what was up with all of the closed stores. Once her loud laughter had slowly subsided, she said with tears in her eyes: "Once again, yet another American has fallen for that big store sign! Heehee-heehee."

When she gradually realized that I was still waiting for an answer, she wiped the tears from her eyes and said: "That just means that the store is open during the lunch-time hours on the days that the supermarket is open. Today is Sunday, and, in contrast to the greedy USA, Sunday means a day of rest. If you want to get something to eat today, you have two options: Either you go to eat at a restaurant or you can get some food at a gas station. Both are only located downtown, and both will cost you dearly."

Upon hearing these words, my tummy marched off in the direction of downtown. I quickly followed. But we never arrived there, for along the way we were led astray, seduced by a certain *Kebab*, with the first name of *Döner*. Resistance was futile. I was young. I had little money. I had to feed myself. And the Kebab on the sign just looked so nice. Hanging out with his mustachioed smiling buddy in his white cooking outfit, the Döner-Kebab looked so inviting. On this very day, a short and passionate relationship began. In the hour when I could find help nowhere else in Germany, Döner Kebab was always there for me. He gave so much, and asked for so little. Normally only five and a half German marks. With or without zaziki.

When I returned home that afternoon much earlier than expected, Frau Wilbärt was still working in her garden. She looked at me with an examining eye and said "Yet again another student seduced by that cursed Döner Kebab." She then sniffed at me from a safe distance and continued: "With zaziki!"

I was slowly getting the impression that Frau Wilbärt was not a very polite elderly lady after all. My suspicion was confirmed upon my signing the rental agreement. As soon as she had this in her hand, she told me: "Herr Bergmann, I don't like your accent." And then she continued: "At least you don't say much, and what you do say I hardly understand anyway." Well, when one has a small vocabulary it is hard to be effusive. On the hand, my landlady loved to hear the sound of her own voice. I believe she actually enjoyed having an attentive young listener in me. It seemed that in some ways we actually fit together fairly well. She was curious and hard-of-hearing, whereas I was curious and "hard-of-speaking".

Frau Wilbärt was proud of her house and her yard. Even though I smelled of zaziki, she deigned to show me her garden. At the end of the tour, she asked me if I had ever seen such a beautiful oasis of green. My attempt to praise her botanical abilities was not completely successful: "Your garden is indeed very beautiful. Almost as beautiful as the exceptionally pretty gardens on the edge of the city where the poor people of the city live in their little huts." She looked at me confused, reflected a moment, looked at her garden and then sighed: "You mean that my garden is almost as beautiful as the 'Schrebergärten'?! Herr Bergmann, where the Schrebergärten are located, is NOT the slums. It is rather a green getaway for the city dwellers who live in apartments and yet would like to have their very own plot of nature." Our conversation thereby was unexpectedly quickly concluded, as she walked off back into the house without a word. (At least at that brief conversation I never again for a moment forgot the meaning of the "Schreber Gardens"!)

Seldom before had I looked forward so much to a Monday morning. During the night I had dreams aplenty about the world famous German bread. Bright and early at 7:00 a.m. I stood in front of the entrance of the bakery next to the supermarket which had disappointed my so bitterly the day before. I had to wait a bit, since an older lady had evidently gotten up even earlier than me and was being served first. While she ordered various types of bread, I eavesdropped intently, eager to learn how to order bread inconspicuously in Germany. The entire procedure seemed at first sight to be more or less doable. I didn't even need to know the names of the various types of bread, or better yet, even whether they were masculine, feminine or neuter. I just had to point at the respective type of bread and say things like: *"Ich hätte gern eins von denen"* (I'd like one of those.) Or *"Ich nehme zwei davon"* (I'll take two thereof.)

But then came a big shock. With a sweet smile, the elderly lady said to the saleswoman: "And last of all, I would like a yummy *'Amerikaner'*." Since this was the German word for "American", I kept quiet and pretended to be a Canadian. Disregarding my rumbling tummy, I crept towards the exit. But then I saw that the lady just got a sugary looking cookie-like pastry to put into her bag. Relief! Since then I can better empathize with how Danes must feel in American bakeries. Or how Hamburgers, Wieners, and Frankfurters must feel all over the USA. (A "*Wiener*", but the way, is actually the German word for "a person from Vienna".)

Then it was my turn. The saleswoman behind the counter noticed quickly by the clueless look in my eyes that, though I might be an academic, I certainly wasn't yet a student of the finer aspects of German bread. And thus I was given a short introduction into the art of German bakeries. Bread, she stated, is not simply bread. There is *"Weißbrot"* (white bread), *"Graubrot"* (gray bread) and *"Schwarzbrot"* (black bread). Yes there is even *"Grünbrot"* (green bread), at least when clueless students from strange lands leave *"Weißbrot"* on the kitchen shelves for over two weeks. She even allowed me to taste-test several types of bread for free. As expected, the *"Weißbrot"* tasted superb, but, in spite of its slightly unappetizing sounding name, the *"Graubrot"* was even tastier. However, the sight of the *"Schwarzbrot"* gave me pause, since it just looked so heavy. My first thoughts were that *"Schwarzbrot"* would actually be better suited as material for the bullet-proof vests worn by police officers. ...

I wasn't prepared for that kind of bread: We may have black bread in the USA, but normally only when we have forgotten to turn off the toaster in time. On the other hand, "Wonder Bread" is much more well-known. (There is now something similar in Germany by the name of *"Toastbrot"*.) Wonder Bread's popularity is due in no small part to its ability to by squeezed into a tiny ball and then weeks later, when needed, to be "pumped" back up to its original size.

Thanks to the student dormitory nearby, the baker-woman evidently knew how to handle nervous looking American students. She carefully handed me a slice of *"Schwarzbrot"* topped with a piece of fresh cheese. Skeptically, I sniffed at the bread offered up to me before opening my mouth.

Then came the delicious moment of whole-grain taste-testing truth. The transformation only lasted a few seconds, but it took place, and it was complete. Since then I am surprised that American bread is still even allowed to be categorized as bread alongside *"Schwarzbrot"*. Satisfied with my reaction, the baker-woman told me that a loaf of *"Schwarzbrot"* has about the nutritional value of two truckloads of "Wonder Bread". This wasn't the only thing that I bought. Before I had moved to Germany, I had heard stories about Germans who had lived happily for years in the USA, but then suddenly felt compelled to move back to Germany, since they just couldn't handle American bread any more. Up until then, I seriously doubted these legends, but now I believed them unreservedly!

Like many Americans, in the USA I rarely go to bakeries, since the bread is often not all that great, and the sweet pastries pack a sugar-shock punch. But in this German bakery there was only one slight disappointment in store for me: the baker-woman's unreflected answer to my question whether the *"Schwarzbrot"* was self-made *("selbst gebacken")* Her reply: "Yes, of course! But not by us."

13: Preferred Prefixes

Considering their position at the forefront of the German language, it is no wonder that these prefixes are called *"Vorsilben"* (literally: "fore-syllables") in German. For though they may be small, these little catalyzers can bring about fantastic effects. As such, they remind me somewhat of the tiny tug-boats in the Hamburg Harbor which can determine the direction taken by the very largest ships of the world. In a similar manner, these few letters can work miracles with German words, as these examples demonstrate:

Un-
When this prefix shows up, the direction of the German language can be immediately thrown into reverse. For instance, an *"Unglück"* (literally: "un-luck") is, after all, not simply the opposite of *"Glück"*, it is a catastrophe! An *"Unwetter"* (literally: "un-weather") is not just bad weather, the roofs of buildings are possibly being blown through the air. When someone does an *"Unding"* (literally: "un-thing"), that person might have to be made *"dingfest"* („arrested"). Moreover, the word *"unverschämt"* (literally: *"un-bashful"*) is not just some poor behavior, it could be a matter of the highest impudence! And lastly, an *"Unwort"* (literally: "un-word") is not just a word which does not exist, but rather a word that shouldn't be spoken of in the light of day!

Ge-
The mighty prefix *"ge"* seems to be the hardest working prefix in the German language, as it shows up just about everywhere. This prefix not only is used to form the passive voice and the past-perfect-tense – even if those tasks alone would be enough for such a small prefix. For instance, the attachment of a "ge"

to the front of a noun implies that something happens quite often. Perhaps even a little too often as can be seen by the following examples: *"das Geschrei"* (clamor), *"das Getue"* (ado), *"das Gebell"* (racket), *"das Gelächter"* (guffawing) etc. It can also signify a bunch of elements, such as *"das Gehölz"* (grove), *"das Gelände"* (terrain), *"das Gestein"* (rock formation), *"das Getier"* (beast) etc. Furthermore, sometimes when the *"ge"* prefix is added, the meaning of the word-stem is altered just slightly, so that German has a nuance of meaning at its disposal which perhaps no other language has. For example, the addition of a *"ge"* to the German word for "bones" (*"Beine"*) transforms it to the meaning of "mortal remains" (*"Gebeine"*).

Ur-

New, previously unsuspected powers can be unleashed from words by means of this prefix. For instance, the *"Urknall"* (Big-Bang) was not just a loud *"Knall"* (bang), but rather the bang that got everything going. When someone is *"uralt"* (old as the hills), then he is not much younger than the *"Urknall"*. An *"Urweib"* is not only a good *"Weib"* (wench), but rather the figurative mother of all women. An *"Urschrei"* (primal scream) is not simply a loud *"Schrei"* (scream), but rather what a man is likely to emit when he is in bed with a *"Urweib"*. *"Urkomisch"* is so much more than just very *"komisch"* (funny). And an *"Urtyp"* is not just an exemplary *"Typ"* (guy), but rather the ultimate guy: So to speak, a man "to the power of '*Ur*'."

Erz-

The words conjured up by this prefix aren't in the least bit wimpy. According to German grammar books, this prefix strengthens the meaning of an adjective in a negative fashion. This can be seen by the examples *"erzfaul"* (lazy to the bone), *"erzdumm"* (dumb as a box of rocks) and *"erzkonservativ"* (conservative without compassion). This also seems to be the case for *"Erzlügner"* (big-time liar), *"Erzfeind"* (arch-enemy) or *"Erzverbrecher"* (serious criminal), but one shouldn't perhaps say this to a *"Erzbischof"*, (arch-bishop) *"Erzvater"* (patriarch) or *"Erzengel"* (arch-angel).

Zer-

Tacking this prefix onto a German word imbues it with a healthy dose of that mythical Germanic toughness in a similar manner to way that the umlauts do: Suddenly the words looks tougher and cooler. Native English speakers can get understandably envious here, since the English language simply does not have an equivalent. One doesn't even need to be able to speak a word of German to suspect at first sight that these words have absolutely nothing to do with simple pleasantries: *"Zerrüttungsprinzip"* (principle of disruption), *"Zermürbungskrieg"* (war of attrition), *"Zerstörungswut"* (destructive fury), *"Zerreißprobe"* (tensile test), *"Zersetzungsprozess"* (degradation process) or *"Zertrümmerung"* (fragmentation). Even the prefix *"zer"* all by itself can form a powerfuly nasty verb: *"zerren"* (a mixture of twitch, tear, tug and yank).

Er-

This elevated prefix signifies either the beginning of an action or the transition from one state of existence to another. In the case of the beginning of an action, the prefix graces the word-stem with a certain amount of style. When one *"erblickt"*, *"erduldet"* or *"ergreift"* something, then one is doing it in a different manner that simply when one *"blickt"* (catch sight of), *"duldet"* (tolerate) or *"greift"* (grasp) that same thing. Or should a flower *"erblühen"*, then it is so much more than any run-of-the-mill *"blühen"* (blossoming). In the case of the transition to another state, this prefix has a similar effect: Should one not only have *"gearbeitet"* (worked) a lot, but also accomplished a great deal, then one has *"erarbeitet"* something. And when one has mastered the useage of this considerable prefix, then one has not only *"gelernt"* (learned) German, but rather *"erlernt"* German. This prefix plays a decisive role in the most important transition of them all in life: death. I often wonder why Germans like the "German" word *"gekillt"*, when this action can be expressed so much more precisely with real German words such as *"erdolchen"* (stab to death by a dagger), *"erstechen"* (stab to death by a knife), *"erschlagen"* (beat to death), *"erschießen"* (shoot to death), *"erwürgen"* (choke to death) etc. Thanks to the addition of the *"er-"* everyone knows immediately what has transpired causing someone to expire.

Voll-

This prefix can have one of two very powerful effects on a word. On one hand, it can strengthen the word-stem, as in *"Vollidiot"* (complete idiot), *"Vollgas"* (pedal to the metal) or *"Volltreffer"* (bull's eye!). This is also evident in one of my favorite German sentences: *"Die Vorlesung war voll leer"* (The lecture was fully empty). On the other hand, the prefix can also completely transform the meaning of a word-stem, as is the case with words such as: *"vollblütig"* (thoroughbred), *"vollkommen"* (complete), *"Vollkraft"* (full of vigor) and *"volltönend"* (sonorous). It goes without saying that one ought to be careful using these four powerful letters! Otherwise, as they say in German, *"Du könntest es voll daneben vollbringen."* (You could end up fully off-target.)

***

Many Americans newly arrived in Germany get the feeling that they can hardly turn around without bumping into something. In contrast to the wide-open landscapes of America, an American in Germany can sometimes get the impression that everything is cramped and full. This feeling overcame me as well when I took a closer look at the tiny refrigerator in Frau Wilbärt's "broom-closet-apartment". I wondered aloud: How am I supposed to squeeze my groceries for the next two weeks into that tiny fridge?

In order to prepare myself mentally and physically for my upcoming bargain-hunting expedition, I decided to first jump under the shower. There I had a flash of inspiration which could possibly solve my dilemma regarding the mini-fridge: I could actually go grocery shopping every other day! For a man from the "land of unlimited refrigerators" this was giant leap of logic. Eureka!

Once I was finished showering and had pulled the shower curtain to the side, I noticed to my chagrin that the bathroom floor was all wet. Evidently I had been so lost in thought that I did not notice that water was getting all over. I tried my best to quickly mop everything up with various towels before Frau Wilbärt caught wind of what had transpired. After all, should that happen, I'd probably quickly be bathed in sweat once again.

I then ran downhill to the supermarket, where the next surprise awaited me: To my astonishment, the grocery carts were chained together. In order to release them from their bonds, I had to pay a ransom of one D-Mark in cold, hard coinage. I thought to myself: If I have to go shopping daily, this is going to get expensive for me. I began to suspect that this was all some sort of conspiracy between the supermarkets and the manufacturers of the tiny fridges.

Once inside, I wanted to buy my very first German magazine. It seemed to me that in Germany a newsmagazine is apparently not taken seriously unless there are half-naked women depicted in some manner on the cover. In fact, evidently there is only one thing better than that on a German newsmagazine: totally naked women. And not only are these magazines in clear sight at every newsstand, but they are also in easy reach of everyone, even kids! This is in complete contrast to the USA, where magazines like Playboy are kept behind the counter, where they are protected by a sullen sales-lady, a plastic cover, and sometimes even by barbed-wire.

It is frequently claimed that there is too little innovation and creativity in Germany, but when I see how serious newsmagazines like *Der Spiegel* and *Stern* time and time again somehow manage to illustrate dry topics by the use of semi-naked women, I no longer worry about Germany's creative spirit. Clearly the most creative of the German newspapers is the *"Bild Zeitung"*. Since it is so omnipresent, I decided to buy myself a copy. After scanning through it, I became even more confused as to its popularity. I had the impression that the only completely undisputed statement in the entire newspaper was the name of the paper itself, which translated into English would be the rather odd-sounding "The Picture Newspaper".

My first trip to the market turned out to be a tough endeavor. Things took such a long time since I had to read all of the food labels so carefully, but fortunately these labels often contained colorful depictions of the items contained within. By the end of my first foray into the supermarket hunting grounds, I was satisfied with the bounty of goods piled up in my shopping cart. But the next shock was already waiting for me at the checkout counter. After the checkout lady had scanned my purchases, she flung them down into a small but steadily growing pile at the end of the counter. I stood there patiently and waited for the "Bag-Boy" to arrive who would quickly, competently and courteously bag my groceries. After all, that was how I was used to things back in the USA. Of course, no Bag-Boy arrived on the scene, and the people in the waiting line behind me gave me increasingly confused and impatient glances. When I asked the checkout lady where my *"Beuteljunge"* was hiding (I simply translated "Bag-Boy" into German, which clearly did not help matters), she recognized my accent and replied: "You are no longer in the USA, young man. Here you have to bag your own stuff yourself!"

Fortunately, I was fairly adept at this task, for I myself had been employed in the Bag-Boy-Business as a youth for a summer. During that time I raked in the grand wage of 2.85 dollars per hour plus tips. When I pointed out to the store manager back then that the minimum wage amounted to 3.35 dollars an hour, he simply replied: "I realize that that is a starvation wage, but you Bag-Boys can all take home any damaged groceries you may find while you are working." After this declaration, there was inexplicably suddenly a marked increase in the amount of damaged goods at the store. As a result, it seemed that not only the Jell-O was not the only food product shaking when we Bag-Boys strolled on past the shelves down the aisles …

Even worse than the miserly wages, though, were the temperature fluctuations when we pushed the carts stuffed with bagged groceries from the 65 degree air-conditioned supermarket out into the 105 degree heat simmering above the black asphalt parking lot. Of course, we complained about this to our boss, but when it came to touching the temperature setting on the air-conditioner, the boss was not listening to any proposals from us. After all, he was comfortably cold in his office. And, as is the wide-spread custom in America, he didn't want to just slightly modify the local climate, he wanted to dominate it. I suspect that it was during that time when I developed my aversion to American air-conditioning. Whenever I start getting melancholy in German supermarkets, because I miss having courteous Bag-Boys at my beck and call, I take consolation in the fact that at least the air-conditioners in Germany are not set on "American-Artic".

Almost as fast as I used to run back home from the grocery store with my daily collection of damaged groceries years ago, here in the German supermarket I speedily packed my goods into the bags which I found myself forced to purchase. But then I got a pleasant surprise: once I dropped off my shopping cart at the exit by hooking up its chain to its fellow carts, my shiny D-Mark popped back out and into my hand. So astonished was I that I almost reflexively made a wish.

Similarly to the experiences of foraging men since the dawn of time, however, my hard-won good-spirits quickly disappeared upon my return to the impatiently waiting woman back at home. Frau Wilbärt stood in the entrance with the sopping wet towels in her hand and a stern countenance on her face. She said: "Herr Bergmann, when it comes to shower curtains, it is clear that you do not understand the difference between 'wasserdicht' (water tight) and 'wasserabweisend' (water resistant)." After her lengthy admonishing, I never again for one second forgot the difference.

Frau Wilbärt took this opportunity to explain a few more of the house rules to me. In conclusion she said: "But I am prepared to perhaps forget this "watery mistake" if you would do me a small favor: I need some drinking water." I cast a confused glance at the water tap, upon which Frau Wilbärt gave me a disgusted look. With a dismissive wave of her hand, she explained: "Nein, das ist 'Fusswasser'!" (No, that is footwater!). I was obviously not following her, so she continued: "Drinking water is something found in bottles at the supermarket. And don't forget: The drinking water in my house needs to contain bubbles! Lots of bubbles!"

After a bit of searching in the supermarket I found a crate

which seemed to fit Frau Wilbärt's description; at least the label implied that the water was imbued with lots of *"Luft und Liebe"* (air and love). I hauled the crate to the check-out counter where the lady on duty demanded more money from me than the price-tag of the water had indicated. I confusedly requested an explanation. She replied that the extra amount pertained to the deposit for the empty bottles and crate. (In German, these are referred to collectively as *"Leergut"* or literally "empty good".) While I searched in my other pants pocket for some more change, I began to wonder why Germans called this *"Leergut"*, but I was already holding up the waiting line so much that I didn't have the courage to pose any more questions.

Along the way back to the apartment, however, it finally occurred to me: Hauling a full crate of water up a hill is truly the opposite of what the Germans would call *"voll gut"*! (full good)

14: One Auto, two "Äuto"?

In second place on the list of the most difficult aspects of learning the German language (after the choice between " *der*", "*die*" and *das*") is for most people remembering the plural forms of words. The possibilities of forming plurals in German are so diffuse that they are even quantified and classified differently by German grammar books. Depending upon the grammar book, there are somewhere between four and twelve alternatives. (This is due to several forms sometimes being grouped together, probably so that the beginning student doesn't give up in despair right at the very start.)

These "dirty dozen" of plural possibilities are as follows:

1. Nothing gets added: e.g. one *"Mädchen"* – two *"Mädchen"* (girls)
If you hear a German man say *"Die Mädchen finde ich hübsch!"* („I think the girls are cute.") Then you only can know that he is talking about several girls if you remember that one girl would be *"das Mädchen"*.

2. An umlaut gets added: e.g. one *"Bruder"* – two *"Brüder"* (brothers)
Even if native English speakers tend to be big fans of umlauts, this plural possibility in German can be problematic. For instance, it took me ages to be able to hear the difference between *"Mutter und Tochter"* (mother and daughter) and *"Mütter und Töchter"* (mothers and daughters).

3. An umlaut and an *"e"* get added: one *"Kran* – two *"Kräne"* (cranes)
Sometimes I have to be careful not to get carried away by this plural option after seeing plural forms like *"Hand und Hände"*.

For the Germans only get confused when I take words such as *"Radio"*, *"Zoo"* and *"Kanu"* and try to pluraize them as follows: *"Rädioe"*, *"Zööe"* and *"Känue"*. (Correct would be *"Radios"*, *"Zoos"* and *"Kanus"*.)

4. An umlaut and an *"er"* get added: one *"Haus"* – two *"Häuser"* (houses)
Here a German learner needs to take care, for although the plural of the word *"Land"* may be *"Länder"* the plural of *"Deutschland"* is NOT *"Deutschländer"*.

5. An *"er"* gets added: e.g. one *"Kleid"* – two *"Kleider"* (dresses)
This manner of forming the plural is not so hard for German words such as *"ein Bild, zwei Bilder"* (one picture, two pictures) and *"ein Kind zwei Kinder"* (one child, two children) but it really gets confusing when Germans translate "two cheerleaders", the big globalplayers", "several insiders", and "the movers and shakers", into German as *"zwei Cheerleader"*, *"die großen Globalplayer"*, *"einige Insider"*, and *"die Mover und Shaker"*. I mean, what happened to the practical "s" at the end of each plural?

6. An "e" gets added: e.g. one *"Stift"* – two *"Stifte"* (pencils)
Theoretically, adding an "e" to make a plural is not that complicated. Unfortunately, sometimes an "e" gets added at the ends of nouns in German for completely unrelated reasons, for instance in the dative case. This phenomenon can be observed in one of the very first expressions that most people learn in German *"zu Hause"* (at home). House may be *"Haus"* in German. But when you are at home, you are *"zu Hause"* even if there is only one house!

7. An "n" gets added: e.g. one *"Kugel"* – two *"Kugeln"* (bullets)
This plural form is theoretically also fairly straightforward, but it alas can get similarly tricky, as sometimes a "n" also gets added to German words for completely different reasons. For instance, "two houses" in German may be *"die Häuser"*, but if you are in them, then you are in *"den Häusern"*.

8. An "en" gets added: e.g. one *"Bett"* – two *"Betten"* (beds)
In some ways, this plural form seems vaguely familiar to native English speakers, probably because we learned as children that the plural form of the English word "ox" is "oxen". However, in German it gets used a lot more often.

9. An "nen" gets added: e.g. one *"Lehrerin"* – two *"Lehrerinnen"* (female teachers)
Actually, this option for making a plural form is relatively simple to learn. But one could still improve upon it. For example, in German a woman from Finland is a *"Finnin"*. And two are *"Finninnen"*. But when there are eight of them present, then shouldn't one actually be surrounded by *"Finninninninninninninninnen"*, instead of just *"Finninnen"* as the grammar books prescribe? (This, by the way, is a pretty mental picture!)

10. An "-s" gets added: e.g. one *"Park"* – two *"Parks"* (parks)
Among most German learners, this plural-forming-possibilty enjoys the most popularity. After all, it corresponds with the manner employed by many other languages such as English and Spanish. This form is not just found with foreign words such as *"Restaurants"*, *"Ufos"* or *"Babys"*. Germans also use it for quintessentially German words such as *"Omas"* and *"Opas"* (Grandmas and Grandpas). And the family *"Löwenzahn"* doesn't consist of the *"Löwenzähne"*, but rather the *"Löwenzahns"*.

11. An "-se" gets added: e.g. one *"Erlebnis"* – two *"Erlebnisse"* (experiences)
As soon as one has adequate *"Kenntnisse"* (knowledge) about this possibility of forming the plural, then one has fewer *"Besorgnisse"* (concerns) and *"Wagnisse"* (perils).

12. It depends: e.g. one *"Organismus"* – two *"Organismen"*, ein *"Museum"* – two *"Museen"*
In the twelfth category are contained all sorts of foreign words for which the plural forms are as varied as the homelands of the words themselves. Examples are words such as *"Agenda"*, *"Globus"*, *"Komma"*, *"Praktikum"* and *"Visum"* – international words which require no translation here into English to be understood. But even if this category doesn't necessary make learning German any easier, it does have at least one huge advantage. Since even Germans have a tough time with them, they tend to have a greater sense of compassion for poor German learners who inevitably make mistakes when forming plurals.

In light of this surplus of plural-possibilities, a person learning German sometimes can't help but wonder aloud: "Does it have to be that way?" Unfortunately, the answer for the German language is *"ja"*. Actually, this is true for all Germanic languages such as Swedish and Dutch. (This could be one of the major reasons why the ancient Romans distrusted the Germanic barbarians so...) In English, the plural is normally formed by adding an "s" at the end of a word, but we also have a few exceptions, such as deer (deer), child (children), man (men), foot (feet) and goose (geese), all of which are old words of Germanic origin.

It must be particularly difficult to learn German for someone who doesn't have a Germanic mother tongue, but instead something completely unrelated, such as Indonesian. In this language, forming plurals is much simpler. For example, a human being is an *"orang"*, two humans are *"dua orang"* and an indefinite number of humans are *"orang-orang"*. (Only in exceptional cases or a few doublings does the word get a new meaning. For instance, *"mata"* means eye, whereas *"mata-mata"* means spy, which I find to be more cute than difficult.) The written forms are similarly uncomplicated, as one need not write out *"orang-orang"*, but can instead choose *"orang"*. Instead of having to deal with complicated forms such as *"Bäumen"* (trees) and *"Häusern"* (houses), if one only had to learn words like *"BaumBaum"* and *"HausHaus"*, then learning German would definitely present fewer *"Problem2"*.

***

During my intensive TV-studies in Göttingen, I really would have appreciated such a simplification of the German language. My TV-studies, however, quickly came to an end, as the day of rekoning had arrived. I sat one autumn day in a large lecture hall on the university campus and took a look around me. In some ways it felt like I was in a United Nations building in New York, as there were people gathered there from all over the globe, and all of them had the same goal: to peacefully make progress forward.

I introduced myself in German to the young man seated next to me and asked him his name and where he came from. He replied: "I am Juri from Königsberg." I responded that I had never before met anyone from Kaliningrad, to which he exclaimed astonishedly: "What kind of American are you, who knows where Kaliningrad is located? Are you some sort of spy?" (Königsberg was the name of Kaliningrad until the Soviet army expelled its German inhabitants at the end of WWII.)

Juri was with me in several German classes later where I

learned to appreciate his sense of humor. But not today, the day of the German test. I was too nervous. Besides, Juri seemed to know way too much about the German language for my tastes. He could even make clever puns in German, such as: *"Wenn hinter Fliegen Fliegen fliegen, fliegen Fliegen Fliegen hinterher."* (When flies fly behind flies, flies fly behind flies.) I could barely keep up with him linguistically and I had to ponder quite a while to figure out exactly just how many flies were actually involved in that sentence. When I asked Juri whether he was nervous about the test, he replied: *"Einigermaßen ..."* While I looked up the word *"einigermaßen"* (somewhat), Juri cheerfully rhymed along with some grammatically questionable sentences such as: *"Wer nicht gut schreibt, der nicht hier bleibt."* (He who writes poorly, he won't last long here.)

In order to gain some self-confidence while the sheets of the written examination were being handed out, I thought back upon the many new experiences which I had made in the previous several weeks. This helped to give me the necessary courage that day.

The test continued the following day with the oral portion of the examination. In the waiting room I ended up once again with Juri next to me. As on the previous day, I asked him whether he was worried. His answer this time: *"Gewissermaßen."* While I was busy looking up the word *"gewissermaßen"* (also "somewhat"), he explained cheerfully with yet another uniquely worded sentence: *"Wir können gut schnacken, wir kriegen's gebacken."* (We can chat well, we'll get it done.)

The "interogation" lasted only about 15 minutes, and I employed my very best TV-German. However, I did decide to refrain from casting any come-hither glances. A few hours later, I got the results: *"Bestanden!"* (Passed!)

It was good that I had concluded my TV-studies before I received my first telephone bill from the *Deutschen Telekom*. Up until then I hadn't actually been sure what Adelheid had meant when she claimed that lots of telephoning was a fiscal impossibility. After all, at that time in the USA telephoning had long since been affordable. But I will never forget my first German telephone bill. It was October 1996 and I was happy simply to have received a letter in the mail. However, I should have suspected something foul was afoot when Frau Wilbärt handed the letter over to me with such a malicious looking grin on her face. Fortunately, I waited to open the letter until I was back up in my room. This had the advantage that I was standing in front of my bed when I almost passed out upon catching sight of the amount that I owed the *Deutsche Telekom*.

Since I suspected a mathematical miscalculation, I called the telephone number stated on the invoice. But instead of reaching a human being on the other end of the line, there was just an answering machine message. As I had expected at least a few comforting words, I was deeply disappointed when the voice explained to me, with apparent glee, what the concept of a monopoly position truly means.

Not until I met up with Adelheid the following weekend did I fully comprehend the "facts of life" when it came to telephoning in Germany in 1996. She handed to me the *Deutschen Telekom's* official "Table of Telephone-Tariffs". It was madness. Even though I normally enjoy tables and graphs so much that my friends sometimes shake their heads in disbelief, I needed some time until I could come to grasp with this monster. Apparently, the world had been divided by the *Deutsche Telekom* into the following zones: *City, Regio 50, Regio 200, Fern, Euro 1, Euro 2, Welt 1, Welt 2, Welt 3* as well as *Welt 4*. Furthermore, for each geographical zone there were the following tariffs for various times of the day and night:

"Mondscheintarif" (moonlight-tariff), *"Freizeittarif"* (free-time-tariff), *"Vormittagstarif"* (morning-tariff) and *"Nachmittagstarif"* (afternoon- tariff).

Now at last I understood what the cheerful voice on the answering machine had meant by the "advantages of a monopoly", for there was the price in black and white: a one hour conversation with someone in the USA at a not ungodly hour costs DM 86.40 in cold, hard cash. For such a stately sum, I would have expected a slightly more appropriately gloomy designiation, perhaps something along the lines of *"äußere Planetenumlaufbahn-Zone 3 zum Weltunter-gangtarif 2"* (outer planetary orbit zone 3 at end of the world tariff 2).

PS. The plural form of *"Mehrzahl"* (plural) is *"Mehrzahlen"* which not only translates into English as "plurals" but also as "to pay more". This is something that I pondered upon each time the telephone bill from the *Deutsche Telekom* came fluttering in to my mailbox during the early months of my stay in Germany.

15: German Levity of Brevity

Contrary to popular opinion, German is not only the language of eternally long words and sentences. It also has at its disposal a wide array of words which are short, sweet and succinct. In my opinion, these indispensable little wonders could considerably enrich any language of the world:

Doch
There are many Germans who are absolutely convinced that English is the best language in the entire world. Anything that German can do, they claim, English can do better. In order to prove the opposite, I only need employ a single, short German word: *"doch"*. I just quickly and unexpectedly grab a full glass of any drink from my German conversation partner and pretend that I want to take a big gulp out of it. While doing this, I say: "You don't mind, do you?" Even if we have been speaking English up until that point, the German almost invariably exclaims: *"Doch!"* After all, in such a situation there just isn't enough time for the comparably cumbersome English equivalent of "Yes! I do!" consisting of its three words. Besides, with *"doch"* one can stress the last two letters of the word in such a manner that the conversation partner feels more or less psychologically compelled to put back the untouched drink softly onto the table.

Quatsch
The word *"Quatsch"* has several fantastic qualities which the English translations such as "nonsense", "balderdash" or "rubbish" just don't have: It consists of a single syllable, it crackles when correctly pronounced, and, similar to the final consonant sound in *"doch"*, it can be stressed in such a manner that any "buts" are quickly nipped in the proverbial bud.

Jein

"Ja und nein" (yes and no) *"sein oder nicht sein"* (to be or not to be). What more can one want? This word is so practical and efficient that I am baffled that we haven't yet come up anything corresponding in English. The first potential alternative to the unimaginative "Yes and no" would be "Nyes". But I suppose this sounds a little too Russian to have a good chance of success in the USA. Unfortunately, the second potential alternative of "Yo" has already had a different established meaning ever since the actor Sylvester Stallone cried it out during the first Rocky movie. To summarize my feelings on the matter: to *"Jein"* I say yes!

Doof

Similarly to the adorable little umlauts, the word *"doof"* has a certain something innocent about it which makes it hard for people to get upset. This is no mean trick, as *"doof"* is actually a derogatory term. It must have something to do with the inherently positive nature of the word. The ability to use the word *"doof"* to playfully insult someone is something that we native English speakers lack. The closest we can come to it is perhaps the word "silly". In this context, the Germans also have at their disposal the related noun *"Doofheit"* (silliness) and personal insult *"Doofi"* (silly-Billy).

Eben

Whenever I tell Germans that *"eben"* is one of the greatest words in the German language, many of them respond as follows: "But in English you have the word 'exactly'!" To this I reply that the German translation of 'exactly' is actually ,genau'. And after some thought on the matter, every German realizes that there is indeed a huge difference in meaning between 'genau' and 'eben'. In fact, in order to express the powerful meaning of the exclamation *"Eben!"* in English, one would need an entire sentence along the lines of: "That is what I have been trying to tell you the entire time!" Very practical? *"Eben!"*

Of course, in addition to these short, sweet, and succinct little words, there are also lengthy lists of eternally long and cumbersome expressions in German, as I was about to clearly experience during my very first university lecture at a German university.

***

The man on the podium spoke a language which sounded vaguely familiar to me. I had the feeling that it must be a Germanic language, but I wasn't sure. Every so often I could catch a phrase or two, but almost never a complete sentence. These I wrote down as quickly as I could. My pencil was dancing across the page while I looked up vocabulary words as fast as possible. After a while, I had the feeling that steam was coming out of my ears from concentrating so hard. I then asked the brunette student on my left, whom I had met a week previously, what kind of language it was that the man behind the lectern was speaking. She whispered back to me: "That is what is referred to as *'Beamtendeutsch-hoch-zwei'.*" (German officialease to the power of two.)

It was the beginning of October 1996, and I was sitting in my first *"BWL-Vorlesung"* (Business-administration lecture). The professor stood up front and was composing grammatical constructs which seemed more complicated to me than the Russian soul. I had never dreamed that sentences could get so long. It seemed that I often had to wait an eternity until the final verb of the sentence finally made its appearance.

A typical sentence went somewhat along the following lines: *"Die in der Presse heiß umstrittene und in weiten Kreisen der*

Öffentlichkeit mehrfach diskutierte Vereinfachung des Wirtschaftsprüfungsver-ordnungsreformgesetzes, das kurz vor dem Ende der letzten Legislaturperiode knapp die Genehmigung verloren hatte, ist in der gestrigen Sitzung des Bundesaus-schusskomitees, das vor einem Monat nach einer immer wieder verlängerten Renovierungsphase in das neu eröffnete Regierungs-gebäude am östlichen Rande des Stadtzentrums eingezogen war, im Einklang mit den Erwartungen der meisten Experten ... bla, bla, bla." (not really worth translating...) Even if I had understood every word, by the end of such a long sentence I would hardly have known more about the core message entailed than I had at the beginning. This phenomenon reminded me of a quotation by Mark Twain: "I didn't have enough time for short letter, so instead I wrote a long one."

In order to combat my increasing drowsiness while the sentence meandered on and on, I turned around and looked over the auditorium. In the back of the room I saw Juri, who seemed like he was about to conclude bets with two fellow Russian students regarding the conclusion of ongoing sentence. Only with a deal of effort was I able to redirect my concentration back towards the front of the room where I had the impression that the sentence was slowly drawing to a close: *"Bla, bla, bla ... zu lautem Beifall der Mehrheit der Anwesenden der Linkspartei, die bei der letzten Wahl zur Überraschung der Führung der CDU wieder in den Bundestag eingezogen war, kläglich gescheitert."* Relieved that the suspense of the sentence had finally been resolved, I gave in to temptation and checked whether among the Russians behind me a few D-Mark bills were exchanging owners.

Once again, I whispered something into the ear of the brunette student on my left side, whose name, by the way, was *"Schnelle Susi"* (Speedy Susi). I asked her what her opinion was of the lecture thus far. After the avalanche of vocabulary during the past hour, I was seriously impressed by the condensed power and feeling wrapped up in one single word she stated: *"Schnarch!"* (Snore!) That a language can express itself either in such long-winded length or in spicy succinctness impressed me considerably. In my search for more knowledge, I asked the dark-haired student to my right, whom I had also met a week prior, and whose name, by the way, was *"Schlaue Susi"* (Savvy Susi), what she thought about the linguistic torrent flowing over us. She said simply: *"Seufz!"* (Sigh!) I quickly caught on and thought to myself: *"Schluck!"* (Gulp!)

My neighbor to the left, *"Schnelle Susi"*, was curious how I was doing in the lecture, and started interrogating me in a whisper. The conversation went – to put it mildly – sub-optimally.

- *"David, sag einfach Bescheid, wenn du hier etwas nicht verstehst."* – *"Bescheid."*
- *"Kommst du überhaupt mit in der Vorlesung?"* – *"Wieso, wohin gehen wir?"*
- *"Das Thema ist schließlich nicht ganz ohne."* – *"Ohne was?"*
- *"Leider waren die Tischvorlagen schon alle."* – *"Alle was?"*
- *"David, also sag mal …"* – *"Mal!"*
- *"Stöhn!"*

(Here the loose English translations:)
- "David, say for certain if you don't understand something." – "For certain."
- „Are you following this lecture?" – "Following it where?"
- "After all, the topic is not all that." – "All what?"
- "Unfortunatley the handouts were all gone." – "Gone where?"
- "David, come on! …" – "On what?"
- "Groan!"

Then she said: *"David, jetzt ist aber Schluss mit lustig!"* (literally: "David, now is a happy ending!") I was really pleased with her statement, at least until the *"Schlaue Susi"* on my right side explained what *"Schluss mit lustig"* really means (Cut the funny stuff!)…

Fortunately, I had already been told during the orientation-session that I ought to bring my binoculars to the lecture if I wanted to be able to see the professor clearly. Let me phrase it this way: Not included among the many dangers of most lectures at German universities is the danger of being overcome by a feeling of loneliness. This has the advantage that the professor hardly notices when one – lulled to sleep by the long sentences – falls asleep in the middle of the lecture. I thus dozed off a bit during the second half of the lecture and dreamt that I, too, would one day be able to speak *"Beamten-deutsch-hoch-zwei"*.

I was roughly ripped out of my pleasant dreams when suddenly a storm broke loose. The transformation was fast, complete and unexpected. One minute I was sitting in the midst of hundreds of student hands writing down notes, the next instant, hundreds of student fists were knocking against the desk tops. Now wide-awake, I thought this action must be a call to rebellion, but instead the others just stood up and departed. I asked my helpful fellow student what the "call to battle" had actually meant. She explained to me that in Germany after lectures people rap their knuckles on the desks as a sort of applause. Most of the German students had already left the hall before I had fully recovered from the shock, but in the front row I saw several Swedes still somewhat shaken, which I found to be mildly comforting. But I did wonder why no one had mentioned this custom during the orientation-session. Ah yes, the small matter of the orientation-session …

Fortunately, the University had reckoned that most of the new students would be slightly disoriented, for the week before the commencement of the lectures was "Orientation Week". Officially I was considered a *"Quereinsteiger"* (transferee), since my American bachelor's degree was recognized as a *"Vordiplom"* (half-way degree), and thus I was permitted to participate in the orientation session for students who had changed their place of studies. There all sorts of mysteries were explained to me – for instance, also why my extremely expensive eight semester studies in the USA was only recognized as a *"Grundstudium"* (preliminary studies) at a free-of-charge university in Germany.

I was already 25 years old, but I did not feel at all out of place in Göttingen, since this seemed to be about the average age of the students there. In the USA, I probably would have qualified for some sort of senior-citizen discount, as there are hardly any students there who have already celebrated their 23rd birthday. In America most young people rush through their time at college, because in this case time literally is money. This was a major difference between the two countries back in 1996. Whereas many Germans were satisfied if they had finished up their studies by the age of 30, many Americans were disappointed if they hadn't made their first million dollars at 30.

Our group at the orientation week consisted of around 15 students, most of whom had come from other universities in Germany. Right off the bat, we had to introduce ourselves to the others in the group. In order to better be able to remember the names of the others, we were instructed to add an adjective to our first name which began with the same letter of the alphabet as our name. This succeeded splendidly. Thus the brown-haired Susi became the *"Schnelle Susi"* and the black-haired Susi the *"Schlaue Susi"*. Also in our midst were, for instance, the *"Rollende Robert"* (rolling Robert), the *"Demolierende Dirk"* (demolishing Dirk), the *"Witzige Wiebke"* (witty Wiebke), the *"Friedliche Friedhelm"* (peaceful Friedhelm), the *"Frauliche Frauke"* (feminine Frauke), the *"Fanatische Frank"* (fanatical Frank) and the *"Bierliebende Birgit"* (beer-loving Birgit).

The mere thought of having to introduce myself in German to the others made me nervous. Especially because all of them evidently spoke German fluently. I considered whether I should introduce myself as *"Der mit dürftigen Deutschkenntnissen David"* (David of the lacking German skills), decided against it, however, and instead named myself the *"Durstige David"* (thirsty David).

The *"Rollende Robert"* told us during his introduction that he came from Croatia. To my ears, however, he sounded like a normal native. He also claimed that German was not his native language. I therefore asked him afterwards what his secret was.

„What do you mean by ‚my secret'?",

„How have you managed to speak German with neither accent nor mistakes?"

"Well, actually I was born in Frankfurt, but my parents were Croatian immigrants ...“

In his opinion, his mother tongue was the language spoken best by his mother. In my opinion this was cheating. To me as an American, he was a German of Croatian decent, or, if he insisted upon it, a Croatian-German. At least, that is how we see things in the USA, where I am a "German-American". My father never would have claimed that he was a German, even if his mother did speak mostly *"Plattdeutsch"* during his childhood.

During the orientation session we were also informed that punctuality at the university was not always taken seriously. In fact, there was even such a thing as the *"akademische Viertel"* (academic quarter). This meant that one could attend certain events 15 minutes after the official start. This was good to know, for up until then I had mistakenly thought that the *"akademische Viertel"* was the part of the city where the professors lived. I was also astonished to learn that, in contrast to my university in the USA, there was no mandatory attendance at the *Universität Göttingen*. I figured that if you don't have to pay for something, then you evidently also don't have to always show up.

Equally very important was the explanation about how the *"Mensa"* worked. In English, the term *"Mensa"* is namely better known as the club which brings all sorts of highly intelligent people under one roof. Now I learned that in German the *Mensa* is a place where all sorts of *"Eintopf"* (stew; literally: "one pot") are served under one roof. The *"Eintopf"* tasted terrific in my opinion, and it was even cheaper than a *Döner!* This was crucial to me, because I was slowly getting an uneasy feeling in my tummy that I shouldn't be subsisting primarily on *Döners...*

During the orientation session I also learned that I could only obtain the designation of *"Diplomkaufmann"* at the end of my studies there. I was disappointed, for I had actually wanted to be able to add the three magical letters of success to my business card: "MBA". Before I had quit my job at the company in Chicago, I had considered whether I should get an American MBA (Master of Business Administration) or rather go abroad for a year in order to obtain a German MBA. Back then I was not yet aware that these three letters would stand for something completely different in German: *"Meister der Beamtendeutschen Ausdrücke"* (Master of German Officialease).

Staun! (My goodness!)

16: By your Command!

At my university in the USA, I had a major and a minor field of studies. My major was in Accounting, because I wanted to be able to get a well-paid job afterwards in order to be able to pay off my huge student loans. My minor, however, was a subject which had always fascinated me: European History. In one of the classes there we read a British history textbook about the First World War in which the following piece of propaganda has stuck in my memory ever since: "The German language has developed itself in order to be the perfect language for the military."

Since I could hardly speak any German at the time, this statement seemed relatively plausible to me back then. After all, the commands given by the German officers in the war movies I had seen certainly sounded precise, succinct, and irresistible. Not until years later, when I had devoted a lot more time to an intensive study of the imperative form in German did I realize that that statement just couldn't hold water. Giving commands in German seemed just too complicated to me.

For instance, when one wants to tell someone else not to forget something, one simple word suffices in English for every single situation: "Remember!" In German, on the other hand, one has to choose between: *"Erinnere dich!"*, *"Erinnert euch!"*, *"Erinnern Sie sich!"* as well as *"Erinnre Dich"* and *"Erinner' Dich"*. The "e" at the end of the German imperative-form can cause a great deal of uncertainty for German learners: Sometimes we are supposed to leave it off, since the word otherwise seems too old fashioned, however, sometimes it needs to be there so that the word is not so difficult to be pronounced.

It gets even harder for a German learner when the strong verbs join the fray. A well-known advertising slogan in English is: *"Just be!"*, which wants to express that one should not get stressed out by society's demands. When trying to express the same in German, however, one can easily get stressed out: *"Sei einfach!"*, *"Seid einfach!"* or *"Seien Sie einfach"*. Another alternative would be: *"Einfach sein"*.

On the other hand, something which probably makes German unique among all of the languages of the world is its ability to express the urgency of a command in a single, concise word by using the *"Partizip Perfekt"* form. For instance, should a German hear the word *"Aufgepasst!"* (Look out!) being yelled out, then the German immediately knows what to do. Unfortunately, this bit of grammar is usually taught rather late in most German classes. My opinion is probably shared, above all, by criminally inclined foreigners. After all, this form, which is relatively seldom used in everyday con-versation, is very popular among police officers. And one should know was is meant when one hears a call of *"Hiergeblieben!"* from behind... (It means: "stop on the spot!")

Fortunately, I got lots of experience with the German imperative form early on during my stay in Germany. After all, in Göttingen I lived in a house where Frau Wilbärt had the final word in any discussion ...

***

At the end of my first month in the broom-closet-apartment I once again heard a knocking at the door. As always, it was Frau Wilbärt. And as soon as I opened the door, I noticed that the situation was serious.

"Herr Bergmann, the month is drawing to a close, and the rent for the next month has to be paid before the preceding month has ended." Obediently I fetched a bunch of dollar bills from my suitcase and laid them out onto the table in front of her, but she just shook her head and said: "A couple of years ago

I might have accepted US-dollars, back then the 'Buck' packed more bang. Nowadays, when it comes to the rent-payment, only money 'Made in Germany' is accepted in this house."

I peered into my wallet to check whether I had sufficient D-Marks therein, but Frau Willbärt stopped me in my tracks with a commanding tone. "No more cash Herr Bergmann! You have to transfer the rent money to my bank account!" Evidently, the first payment in cash had been an exception. I explained to Frau Wilbärt that such a transfer was not possible for me, since I didn't have a bank account. Her response: "Then you had better open one quickly. There are, after all, lots of students in this city who have such a bank account and who would love to rent your room next month from me." Not until she had reached the bottom of the stairwell did the sounds of her land-lady-laughter fade away out of earshot. It was obvious to me that it was high time for me to get banking if I wanted to be able to bank on staying in my new abode.

As such, I made my way into the city in order to open up a bank account. This was just about as difficult as I had expected it to be. My first stop was the Citibank. I recognized that name right away, since it is an American bank, so I thought that I might have a good chance there. At least that is what I hoped for at first... But within its doors were neither countrymen, nor home-field-advantage, nor an account for me. The bank employee explained the situation as follows: "Herr Bergmann, our target customers are people who, in all probability, will not leave the country within the next several months. People who have some money. People who have a job. People who have a German *"Bürgschaft"* (guarantee) at their disposal. Should you one day possess one or more of these characteristics, we could then get down to business." Though I could understand his reasoning, I thought to myself that he shouldn't count on my returning to that bank.

Things went similarly at the other banks. The array of services offered by the *"Spar-da-Bank"* seemed rather straightforward to me, since the name directly translated into English literally means "Save-Here-Bank", but for me it unfortunately became the *"Nix-da-Bank"* (Nothing-Here-Bank). I started to worry that I would soon have to open an account on a park-bench. (In German, the translation of the English words "bench" and "bank" are both *"Bank"*.) But then I struck gold (figuratively) at the bank with its name written in big, bold letters of gold: the Commerzbank.

I was even more surprised when I asked the friendly bank-lady whether I could choose the color and pattern of the checks I would be using (after all, in the USA this is considered to be a special service). Her reply was "Herr Bergmann, you won't need any checks here." My counter-question evidently surprised her even more: "Because I have so little money?" She then proceeded to explain to me how the payment system in Germany functions.

Even if it may be efficient, it took some time for me to fully comprehend the difference between an *"EC-Karte"* and a *"Eurocard"*. (The former is a true "debit-card", something fairly rare back then in the USA, whereas the latter is just a run-of-the-mill credit-card.) As a bean-counter by profession, I was, of course, quite excited that I could print out my bank-statements as often as I wanted, and not wait, as was the case in the USA back then, for my bank statement to come in the mail at the end of the month. With much fanfare, I made my first wire-transfer to the good old Frau Willbärt, and a wave of relief washed over my debt-free shoulders.

Excited like a child on Christmas morning, I withdrew my first cash from the automated teller machine. I was fascinated by the bills themselves. They were colorful and of varying sizes, so very different that the dollar bills in the USA, which are all the same size and shades of green. On the back side of the *"Zehnmarkschein"* (Ten German Mark bill) were depicted some of the sights of Göttingen. I gladly accepted the challenge of locating as many of these as possible myself in the city. Even better, in my opinion, were the hundred D-Mark bills, as Clara Schumann looked simply stunning on them. Unfortunately, our relationship seemed to be a rather one-sided one, for she obviously preferred being seen in the hands of more well-to-do gentlemen.

I wanted to immediately try out my new bills and decided to make a few major purchases. I needed just about everything, since I had only brought as much from the USA as I could stuff into two suitcases. In Göttingen I had been struck early on by how many bikes were about the streets. Especially impressive were the omnipresent bike paths, but even more striking to me was the fact that even many elderly ladies were seen about on their bikes. What a country, I thought to myself! The elderly ladies want to get their money via wire-transfer and they use bikes as a means of transportation in public!

It was therefore completely clear to me what my first purchase should be. After all, I wanted to be able to keep up with the German Grannies when it came to street-speed. Thus I made my way out of the banking district and headed off to the "bike-shop district". In a shady backyard court at the edge of the downtown, I finally found what appeared to be a used-bike shop. The bike-salesman asked me what kind of *"Draht-Esel"* I wanted to buy. I was relieved that I understood both the word *"Draht"* (wire) and *"Esel"* (donkey), but I wasn't sure what they had to do with my situation, so I replied stubbornly in German: "I don't want a "wire-donkey"; I need a bike!", little knowing then that these two items are simply two names for the same item. The salesman didn't comment on my strange reaction, but rather simply smiled. He probably just presumed that with me he probably wouldn't have to haggle too long over the price.

He showed me several bikes broken down (figuratively speaking … mostly) into various categories: "brand-new", "nearly brand-new", "only stolen once", "stolen repeatedly" and a "collection of bike-parts held together tenuously". Since the pricing system apparently was based on the *"Angebot-nicht-Fragen-Prinzip"* (supply and don't demand any explanations principle), it was easy for me to make my decision: I chose an "only stolen once" bike. I believe that I thereby found myself for the very first time in Germany in what the natives call *"Kaufrausch"* (shopping fever).

From then on I felt like an immaculately fearless *"Drahteselritter"* ("Wire-donkey-cowboy"). In order to celebrate, I decided to buy an ice-cream. At the ice-cream shop I therefore ordered in German *"eine Eissahne!"* (little knowing that my literal translation of "ice-cream" resulted in a German word that didn't exist, as in German it is called *"Speise-Eis"* or "dining ice"). So I shouldn't have been so surprised when the ice-cream saleslady dryly answered: "I don't know what *"Eissahne"* is, but we don't have it." I looked over the wide array of ice-creams on selection and thought to myself: "Evidently this is another case of me not understanding something!" Thus, I decided on the silent movie version of ordering: I indicated with my pointer-finger the type that I wanted, then at my mouth, and then laid my money onto the counter. After I had received what I had come for, I backed slowly out of the store with my hard-won treat.

Secure in the saddle of my new "wire-donkey", my journey back to my little chambers no longer seemed quite so long. But the path felt all the steeper! I found it somehow fitting that the street which I had to ride the longest was called *"Nonnenstieg"* (Climb of the Nuns). Nevertheless, I had the feeling that my bike had been a real steal. Unfortunately, already after only one week my bike itself was stolen! Although in many respects it did look like a "*Omafahrrad*" (Grandma-bike), it did have something special: two bike-baskets. As I closely examined the remaining fragments of my broken cheap bike-lock, I came to the conclusion that the thief must simply have been overcome by a case of "*Korbneid*" (bike-basket-envy).

The saddest part of it all for me, however, was that I could no longer whiz through the streets of the city with the fresh air blowing through my hair. Instead, I had to swallow my pride and walk back home to where I had my debit card and my remaining "Claras". Once there, I told Frau Wilbärt of my loss. Her reaction didn't exactly raise my spirits: "Heeheehee! Already after five days your first bike has been stolen! That is a new record time for a tenant in this house!"

After she had wiped the tears from her eyes, she noticed that I was still waiting for an explanation of what had transpired. This she delivered with much joy: First of all, lots of bikes are stolen in Göttingen. Secondly, there is a big difference between the two options when it comes to locking up a bike. These are known in German as "*angekettet*" (locked to something solid) and "*abgekettet*" (just plain locked by itself). "*Angekettet*" with a sturdy lock means that the bike might just stay for a good while. "*Abgekettet*" with a cheap lock (like the one I had used), on the other hand, means quite the opposite: the bike is going bye-bye sooner than one would like.

Even though I never did find my bike in the following days, I was able to quickly come to terms with its loss. After all, the theft also meant something positive for me: another wonderful opportunity for more "*Kaufrausch*"! Besides, I knew what I would yell out to the thief in a commanding voice should I ever see him pedaling on by: "*Runter vom Sattel!*" (Get down off of that saddle!)

17: Cruel Language? Cool Language!

I have often been asked for a few examples of some cool German words. Since the language has so many of them, it is not easy to squeeze a worthy and representative selection into a short list, but here is modest attempt. (Included in parentheses are the more or less approximate translations into English):

- *"Pipapo"* – Take some *"Pi"*, add some *"Pa"*, and then some *"Po"*, and already you've said everything that needs to be said. (odds and ends)
- *"Luxusweibchen"* – Two desirable things combined in one word. (a little lady of luxury)
- *"Tiefstaplerin"* – Even the opposite of a *"Luxusweibchen"* can be something good. (a woman of understatement)
- *"entgegengegangen"* – It is just fun to say a word with so many syllables starting with the letter G. (to have moved towards something)
- *"Stinktier"* – With this word, there is absolutely no doubt what this animal does: it stinks. (skunk)
- *"Schadstoffausstoß"* – This word sounds appropriately menacing. (exhaust pollutant)
- *"Doppeltgemoppelt"* – Twice as cool as most words. (tautology)
- *"Augenweide"* – A truly beautiful word. (a feast for the eyes)
- *"Brisanz"* – The strong opposite of a weak breeze. (explosive power)
- *"Erlauschen"* – To hear everything in fine style. (to listen carefully)
- *"Tatütata"* – The sounds of sirens signifying trouble.
- *"Eichhörnchen"* – An animal's name meaning "little oak-horn" must be adorable. (squirrel)
- *"Hirnrissig"* – When an idea is so bad that it cracks brains. (crazy)

- *"Aalen"* – To luxuriate under the warm rays of the sun like only an eel can. (to bask)
- *"Erquicklich"* – Pleasant AND inspiring: What more could one want? (invigorating)
- *"Tohuwabohu"* – At the mere sight of this word, one senses the chaos behind it. (hullabaloo)
- *"Müßiggänger"* – A person who is somehow actively behaving leisurely. (dallier)
- *"Schlaftanken"* – A *"Müßiggänger"* doesn't doze, he "fills up his sleep-tank". ("power-sleeping")
- *"Inständig"* – One can almost sense the yearning and desire within this word. (ardently)
- *"Lostigern"* – Moving towards a goal with a certain *"Grrrrr"*. (proceeding "tiger-like")
- *"Machtwort"* – So much power in one word. (a word which lays down the law)
- *"Kraftakt"* – So much power in one action. (a show of strength)
- *"Überhaupt"* – ... *und überhaupt!* (not really translatable, but something like "at all")

With so many wonderful words in German, there is almost no end to the linguistic fun to be had! At least that is how things went for me and my dear foreign fellow students in our German language class in Göttingen back in the fall of 1996.

***

"Is this here some sort of university for spies?", asked Juri with a face full of disbelief. "I can't believe that almost everyone here knows where Kaliningrad is located!" The catalyst for his outbreak of astonishment was the comment from Jerome from Paris, when he stated that he had never before met anyone from the city of Kaliningrad. (Jerome refuted not only the cliché of the Frenchman who doesn't speak foreign languages, but also a similarly prevalent one: He was namely extraordinarily humorous.)

Juri was the first one in the class to introduce himself to the group. He came from *Königsberg* and was studying *"Betriebswirtschaftslehre"* or *"BWL"* for short (Business Administration). His hobbies included drinking vodka, fixing broken bikes, playing guitar and singing melancholy songs. We fellow students were impressed above all by his mastery of German slang words, especially when he mentioned that his nickname was the *"Königsberger Klops"*. (Königsberger meat-ball)

We foreign students had been placed into various German classes based on the results of our language tests. At first I wondered if I actually belonged in the same course as Juri. Was it possible that the placement results had been wildly shuffled? Granted, I already had completed several German courses, but these classes here in Göttingen were something completely new for me. In contrast to my previous classes, there were students here from all over the entire world, even quite a few who didn't understand any English. But, no matter where we had come from originally, now we all wanted to learn the German language together. If anything was going to be beaten here, then it would be paths to German linguistic proficiency.

The teacher spoke up in response to Juri's question: "No, Juri, this is not a university for spies. But, do tell, where did you learn German so well?" He replied: "My father was an officer in the Soviet Army. Among other assignments, he was stationed with our family in East Germany for several years where he had a fairly good position. Already back then we could even receive western TV. Communism may have had a lot of drawbacks, but for some Comrades it wasn't all bad."

After Juri, a young woman from Hungary had her turn. She simply stated shyly: "My name is Anna, and I cannot speak German very well." The teacher tried to coax more information out of her, but more was not to be had. After the eloquent dialogue and banter between Juri and Jerome I had begun to seriously doubt my German skills, but my self-confidence rebounded a bit after Anna's brief introduction. (However, when we later got the results back from our first written test in the class, we were astonished to discover just how good Anna's German actually was. She achieved the best test-result in the class by far. Evidently there were rows upon rows of linguistic rules, grammatical constructs and treasure troves of a vocabulary in her head, but she just had difficulties putting them orally into words.)

As far as the German language was concerned, the next student to be introduced was the "Anti-Anna": a young Danish woman named Anke. In contrast to the monosyllabic Hungarian girl, Anke could produce a waterfall of words at the drop of a hat. This impressed us mightily – at least until we gradually noticed that not everything she said was correct, strictly speaking. During a break several weeks later, Jerome confided to me that he had looked up some of Anke's favorite expressions and ascertained that much of what she said was not grammatically possible in German. Apparently she simply translated many idioms directly from Danish into German, which wasn't immediately evident to us, since Danish and German are so similar. In our eyes, Anke was therefore not only what the Germans would call a *"Quasselstrippe"* (motor-mouth), but also on top of that a *"Quatschstrippe"* (nonsense-mouth)!

In our class were also three students from Poland. One of them was a true "cavalier of the old school", even though he was only 24 years old. No matter what the situation was, he seemed to always have a fitting polite phrase in every language at his disposal. The other two Poles seemed to be the complete opposite sort of people. For some reason, I got the vague feeling that they looked like they first wanted to steal my bike so that they could sell it back to me later.

Last, but certainly not least, a young Dutch woman by the name of Nanda took her turn to introduce herself, something that she accomplished completely without a trace of a foreign accent! She spoke such good German that she could often fool actual Germans into thinking she was also a native German speaker. One German man who claimed to be proficient at placing Germans' places of origin on the basis of their accent was frustrated that he couldn't pin-point hers exactly within the Federal Republic, but he was fairly certain that she came from somewhere in Lower Saxony. Jerome and I cast each other an envious look which was easily understandable even without words: no one ever mistook us for Lower-Saxonians!

Even if she wasn't officially the University Head-Mistress, sometimes our German teacher, Frau Tamchina, gave us the impression that she thought she ought to be. Her job of teaching German to us was perfect for her, as it gave her many opportunities to hold long speeches and to philosophize at great length about the nature of the world. We foreigners didn't have a linguistic chance when it came to conversations with her. She could easily transform any dialogues into monologues. By the time that we had finally figured out how to put our response into words, she had already moved on to her next topic. For instance, when Jerome was asked where he came from, he answered Paris. Frau Tamchina immediately seized her chance to exclaim that he was thereby somehow claiming that Parisians feel that Paris is a synonym for all of France! Jerome never got the chance to explain himself, as the teacher had already launched into a soliloquy about the many peculiar characteristics of the Parisians.

Admittedly, it was her duty to bring us out of our linguistic shell. And sometimes she actually brought up some fairly interesting topics. For instance, one day she explained to us that in Germany there is periodically a competition to choose the most beautiful German word. She wanted to know which words we found to be particularly charming, along with, naturally, the reasoning behind for our choices. We found this assignment to be a proverbial piece of cake, since it was obvious to us that there are so many wonderful words. (The list at the beginning of this chapter demonstrates my stance on this matter.) Frau Tamchina particularly enjoyed this exercise, as she could tell by the explanations whether the students truly understood the meanings of their favorite words.

Here are some of her favorite misunderstood words which she had accumulated over her many years of teaching. Next to the popular German words are the correct translations into English, followed by the new and often creatively curious meaning:

- *"Sterbetafel"* – Mortality table. (An executioner's desk of death.)
- *"Entpuppen"* – To turn out to be. (Stealing a man's cute girlfriend, a.k.a. his "Barbie-doll".)
- *"Verdünnisieren"* – To dilute. (What happens to people at a "fat-farm".)
- *"Hexenwerk"* – Rocket-science. (A witch factory.)
- *"Halbleiter"* – Semi-conductor. ("Assistant-Manager", but literally "half-leader".)
- *"Freudenreich"* – Full of joy. (The kingdom next to "The Land of Milk and Honey".)
- *"Uropa"* – A great-grandfather. (Old Europe.)
- *"Verlustieren"* – To amuse oneself. (The opposite of winning.)

In this regard, things were no different in our course. One of the "bike-thieves" from Poland chose the word *"Meerbusen"* – at least until it was explained to him that this a not, after all, a synonym for "a well-endowed woman" (but sounds like: "more breasts") but rather for the German word *"Golf"* (gulf), and not for the *Golf,* which people play nor for the *Golf,* which people drive. Confronted with this revelation, the Pole then instead chose the word *"Zöllehölle"* (customs hell), which was his designation for the border crossing between Poland and Germany.

The two students in our class with by far the worst German skills were two American women aged about 20. They evidently didn't know even some of the most basic vocabulary words. As such, most of the time they simply tried to talk to the other students in English. Since Juri basically didn't speak a word of English, he didn't necessarily appreciate this linguistic treatment. One time he couldn't hold back a frustrated *"Meine Fresse!"* (Bloody Hell!), to which one of the Americans exclaimed: "Hey, I know the word *'Fresse'!* I've seen it written once on one of the toilette stalls!"

The Americans at the university could be divided into two groups: there were those in my age group (mid- to upper-twenties) who had already concluded their studies in the USA and were now here in Germany for an additional degree. Like me, many of them had already worked and were therefore delighted and grateful to have the opportunity to learn a new language and a new culture. We were simply intoxicated by our new found freedoms. On the other hand were the youngsters who were closer to the age of 20. They appeared to be greatly pleased to just be so far away from their parents. They seemed to be intoxicated even more often than we older students were, but for clearly different reasons: chiefly because beer in Germany can be drunk almost everywhere in public.

Some of youngsters had even chosen a German university because they had heard that the world-famous German beer was cheaper than water in its country of origin. Once they discovered, however, how expensive water can be in Germany, they were naturally correspondingly disappointed ...

But whatever our differences, we were all of the same opinion when it came to deciding what the *"Unwort"* ("un-word") of the German language is. It is *"Schlager"* (a category of German folk/rock songs). During their first semester, most of the foreigners tried more or less to fit in to German society. But now and then there were always situations which made clear to us that we would never comprehend certain aspects of "German-ness": For instance, the so-called *"Schlager-*time". At a student-party we would all be dancing away to the songs which were familiar to all of us. But then, in one fell swoop, it was suddenly made abundantly clear who among those present was really a German, and who was actually an imposter. For the natives continued merrily dancing away, whereas the foreigners fled the dance floor – driven off by what they considered to be the bad sounds of a *"Schlager"*. These may be beloved by Germans, but for us they were a clear sign that only two options remained open to us: either to hit the bar for some strong alcohol or to hit the road.

Over the years, the Germans have developed a marked fondness for the English word "Hit" in its capacity to designate a successful song. The word *"Schlager"* on the other hand, seems to be derived from the German word *"Schläger"* (racket). After all, whenever such a song is played it seems to make a loud racket.

Nevertheless, we foreigners tried to keep an open mind and to be receptive to new things, so over the course of the semester we even succeeded in finding a few *"Schlager"* which we found to be not all that bad, for instance the song *"Moskau"* from the band *"Dschingis Khan"*. Only Juri just couldn't come to terms with it, as it sounded to him too much like a parody of his beloved Motherland, Russia. Especially the refrain with its line *"Wirf die Gläser an die Wand. Russland ist ein schönes Land"* (Throw the glasses at the wall. Russia is a beautiful country.) He exclaimed that Russians don't throw their drinking glasses at the walls. Not even the spies do that....

18: Reforming the German Language Reforms

In one of my German grammar books I read the following statement regarding German spelling: "The orthography in German does not completely align with the pronunciation (in contrast, for instance, to the Finish or Turkish languages). Rather, it only closely approximates the sounds. For German spelling also takes into consideration the sentence structure (punctuation), syllable structure (identification of the short vowel sounds), type of word (capitalization of nouns) as well as the uniformity of root-word.

Nevertheless, whenever a person learning German asks a native German speaker how a word is spelled, he or she often gets the answer: *"Wie man es spricht."* (The way it is pronounced.) But since German spelling is only closely approximates the pronunciation (here the Germans have a wonderful word for this characteristic: *"lautfundiert"*), this answer does not help out all that much. For example, in spite of their markedly differing spellings, the names of the two German cities *"Rothenburg"* and *"Rohtenburg"* are pronounced exactly the same!

One encounters a similar problem when trying to determine whether the subject of the conversation is a *"Feilchen"* (little file), a *"Veilchen"* (a violet) or a *"Pfeilchen"* (a tiny arrow). In a different field of conversation, one can't always be certain whether someone has stated that they are *"seekrank"* (they are seasick), *"sehkrank"* (they can't see straight), or *"säkrank"* (they are tired of sowing and finally want to harvest). Once I was seriously confused when I met a northern German woman, as she introduced herself to me by saying: *"Mein Nachname ist Pfau, geschrieben ohne V."* (My name is *"Pfau"*, written without a *"V"*.) Since the word *"Pfau"* (peacock) and the letter *V* are both pronounced basically the same in northern Germany, I thought at first that she was a lady without a last name, somewhat along the lines of Madonna or Cher.

In order to make some "improvements" to spelling in German at the end of the 20th century, the so-called *"neue deutsche Rechtschreibreform"* (New German Spelling Reform) took place. The goal of this reform was not to be major spelling revolution, but rather "a small reform of reason". In July 1996 the states of the German Federal Republic, along with the German speaking countries of Austria, Switzerland and Liechtenstein, committed themselves by means of the *"Wiener Absichtserklärung zur Neuregelung der deutschen Rechtschreibung"* to introducing the new spelling. (Sometime in the 21st century…).

***

When I boarded the plane in September 1996 to fly off to Germany in order to commence with my studies in Göttingen, I didn't suspect that I was on my way into a linguistic firestorm. Since I, at that time, had only been learning German for three short years, I observed the boisterous struggle with a healthy measure of dispassion.

To me, the important questions were as follows:

- Will the nice little letter "ß" be allowed to stay?
- Will any new umlauts be introduced?
- Will it finally be settled whether the spelling of "nightmare" in German is either *"Albtraum"* or *"Alptraum"*?
- If it is called the "New German Spelling Reform", when was the old one, and how did that work out?

In order to get to the bottom of this puzzle, I decided to do some researching over the course of the semester at the

Göttingen university library. There I discovered the following: In 1876 the Prussian government called together a conference in Berlin in order to better unify the German spelling. (I found it noteworthy that this occurred five years after the German unification, just as the "New German Spelling Reform" was introduced five years after the reunification of the country in 1990). The introduction of the new orthography caused quite an uproar in the general public and led to a conflict within the society. Even the German Imperial Reichstag and Prince Bismarck sided with the conservative opposition.

But in spite of all of this, the new "Putkamersche Ortho-graphy" won out in the end. This victory was due in large part to the new "Dictionary of the German Language" put out by Konrad Duden in 1880. The popular school and work-place orthographies contributed to the pressure being put onto other public institutions to update their own spelling. In June 1901, representatives of the 26 German speaking states of central Europe were invited to the *"Zweiten Orthographischen Konferenz"* in Berlin in order to codify the spelling in German on the basis of the Prussian manual.

This subject became somewhat more personal for me when I received a small package in the mail from my father. Inside was a very old German grammar book which he had found while tidying up the attic on the old family farm. Its bilingual title was *"Deutsch-englische Lesebücher für katholische Schulen"* – "German-English Readers for Catholic Schools" (Copyright 1910 by the Benziger Brothers, Cincinnati, Ohio), and on the first page on the inside stood the maiden-name of my Grandma Bergmann: Frances Bruns. Although she was already a member of the fourth generation in America after the immigration by her great-grandparents from Germany, she still spoke Low-German at home and therefore had to learn not only English in school, but also High-German.

In the preface of the book, the significant changes brought about by what back then was also referred to as the "new German spelling" were summarized in six main points. These were as follows:

1. "From now on, the letter combination "TH" is only to be used in foreign words and names."

I suspect that nowadays not even the bitterest opponents of the modern German spelling reform are shedding any tears (*"Thräne"* in the old spelling instead of the modern *"Träne"*) over this matter. After all, the old style spelling of German words such as *"Thon"* (tone), *"Thor"* (gate), *"That"* (deed) and *"Thür"* (door) now look as archaic to German eyes, as "thee and thou" look to modern Americans. Even if the German tongue doesn't distinguish between the T- and the TH-sound, back then (as today) they evidently did not want to change foreign words in this area. Otherwise, my Grandma's book would have been written for *"Katolische Schulen"* instead of *"Katholische Schulen"*. (Catholic schools.)

2. "The letter combination PH (instead of F) is only to be used in foreign words."

Unless, of course, the foreign word has settled in so completely in German that it no longer seems like a foreigner to the natives. Otherwise the Germans wouldn't be writing words like *"Elefant"* and *"Telefon"*.

3. "Almost all words which previously used a C for the K-sound, are now to be written with a K; Those which used a C for the Z-sound are now to be written with a Z."

It is about time! In English, the letter C is causing, now as before, all sorts of mischief.

4. "Instead of AE, OE and UE, one should write simply Ä, Ö and Ü; An exception is to be made for personal names."

This is my personal favorite among all of the changes of the first German Spelling Reform, for through this change, support for the mighty umlauts was further underpinned! Besides, now I finally understood why people learn German in the *"Goethe-Institut"*, and not in the *"Göthe-Institut"*. (Back at the end of the 19th century, clearly no one suspected what kinds of problems the umlauts would one day cause in email addresses.)

5. "The separation of PF, TZ and DT, but not ST at the end of a printed line."

In contrast to most of the participants of the Congress, in this matter I have absolutely no strong opinion.

6. "In cases of doubt regarding the capitalization of nouns, non-capitalization is preferred."

This recommendation regarding capitalization was partly reversed in the new spelling reform.

Even if the discussions regarding the German spelling at congresses and in German courses can sometimes get a bit heated, almost everyone can agree that the irregularities in German are nevertheless basically manageable. Whereas German spelling is more or less based on the pronunciation of the word, in English it sometimes seems to be based instead on pure randomness.

This jumble in English is essentially due the English language being able to trace its roots back to so many sources. Among the various Germanic tribes of the early Middle Ages on the British Isles there were already enough problems with spelling, but when the French-speaking Normans under

William the Conqueror joined the fray in 1066, things only got more muddled linguistically. In the following centuries, two languages co-existed side by side, mixing, mingling and meandering. To top it off, no one seemed to be in charge of this change, as the English language has never had a language oversight-committee like the ones in France or Spain.

Nevertheless, this didn't seem to hinder the spreading of the English language over the globe, with the result that English is nowadays the official language of more countries in the world than any other language.

No small number of Germans seem to derive great pleasure from informing me that I don't speak English at all, but rather "just" American. This joke at my expense is not something which I find all that amusing. Evidently, someone has decided in the German speaking countries to divide the English language into several languages. However, we Americans find this just about as cute as Austrians do when they are told that they don't speak German, but rather "Austrian". Or as Mexicans do when they hear that they only speak "Mexican". Not very cute. This strange division can even be seen in books, clearly written in black and white *"übersetzt aus dem Amerikanischen"* (translated from the American) instead of *"übersetzt aus dem amerikanischen Englisch"* (translated from American English). I wouldn't be surprised if sooner or later I find a book in which it is written in the front *"Übersetzt aus dem Ohioschen"* (translated from the Ohioan).

In Germany I know many Eastern Europeans who learned German as their first foreign language. Although German has more declinations, reflections, and conjugations than English does, in German there are considerably fewer exceptions to the rules. As a German-speaking friend of mine from Siberia likes to say: *"Englisch treibt mich in den Wahnsinn. Die Recht-schreibung ist eine einzige Quälerei!"* (English drives me crazy! The spelling is one exquisite form of torture!) When a person from Siberia states this, then that is really saying something.

One of my favorites of her English spelling mistakes was her long misspelling *"E-Mail"* as: *"I-Mehl"*. This may be how it would be phonetically spelled in German, but that would mean "I-Flour". Nevertheless, she doesn't give up easily, and whenever the topic of "English" comes up, she makes a face, and then counts very proudly from one to twenty. At the end she looks so relieved that I just don't have the heart to tell her that she once again has forgotten the number 13.

I find it rather ironic that the most widely spread language nowadays is such a chaotic one– at least in terms of its spelling. As a member of the prestigious *"Real Academia Española"* once phrased it: "Spanish is order. English is disorder." For instance, the following sentences in English are pronounced almost identically, even though this could hardly be expected at first sight: "I won two ewes." and: "Aye! One to use!"

For this reason, there is a phenomenon in the USA which is completely unknown in German speaking countries: Spelling contests. For some reason unknown to almost everyone, these are called "Spelling Bees", and they are held every year in schools. The winners of each contest continue on and on until, after several rounds, they reach the final round in the nation's capital. Coincidently enough, the final words which both the champion and the first runner-up had to spell in the 2006 Scripps National Spelling Bee were of German origin!

Since the teenager Katharine Close from New Jersey knew how to spell the word *"Ursprache"* (original language), she received the first price of 42.000 dollars. Because the second-place finisher did not know how to spell *"Weltschmerz"* (she started with the letter "V"), she received for all of her hard work a good deal less money. Of course, there were loads of other foreign words in the competition, but during that year's contest the words of German origin were especially well-represented: *Heiligenschein* (misspelled), *Wehrmacht, Bildungsroman, Appenzell* (misspelled), *Ersatz, Langläufer, Schloss, echt, Lebensraum* and *Edelweiss* (misspelled).

Near the end of the semester in Frau Tamchina's German class, we were given the assignment of holding a brief lecture on a linguistic topic of our choice. I decided to choose the topic of the German Spelling Reforms, using my Grandma's very old grammar book as a basis. After my presentation, we foreigners in the class were uniformly of the opinion that we could probably carry out a German Spelling Reform much better that the Germans themselves, since we could view the language more clearly and objectively. Besides, we knew the rules and their exceptions all by name!

Only Frau Tamchina seemed far from convinced by our arguments. Especially as her glance fell upon the two "bike-thieves" from Poland ...

19: From "Ami" to "Zoni"

It does not surprise me one bit that Germans have very merrily borrowed the following words from the English language over the years: Hippie, Party, Hobby, easy, Handy, Rowdy, happy, Lady, Teenie, Pony, Dandy, Lobby, and Junkie. After all, though the German language may be known the world over for its dry and serious words (e.g. "*Schadenfreude*"), Germans also are quite fond of using cute diminutives.

One of the first things taught in most German classes are the uses of the diminutive endings "*-chen*" and "*-lein*". It is not until much later, however, that German-language-learners discover the widespread use of the less well-known diminutive ending "*-i*", despite its ubiquity. Its omnipresence was especially evident during the Soccer World Cup hosted by Germany in the summer of 2006, where one could read in just about all of the newspapers on a daily basis about how *Schumi* and *Angie* were intently watching as *Klinsi*, *Schweini* and *Poldi* were playing "*Fußi*" on the soccer field. Even serious topics are not off-limits for these little diminutives, as German-learners somewhat perplexedly realize, for instance, when they read their first "*Krimi*" (crime novel) about a "*Chauvi*" (chauvenist) and a "*Tussi*" (bimbo) among "*Stasi-Promis*" (Stasi-celebrities) and "*Neonazi-Asis*" (Neo-Nazi-rebels).

At the beginning of my time in Germany, I was uncertain whether I wanted to be called an "*Ami*" (a short form for "*Amerikaner*"). As it turns out, my skepticism was not completely unfounded. The word itself sounds actually kind of harmless, and it reminds me sometimes of the English word "amiable". Moreover, in French it even means "friend". But somehow the word "*Ami*" can get annoying after a while, especially since I have realized that the word is used rather frequently in a somewhat disparaging manner. For example in the sentences: *"Amis haut ab!"* (Yanks go home!) or *"Der Ami hat ohnehin keine Ahnung."* (The Yank doesn't have a clue.) What is worse, it seems that only we Americans have the "honor" of having such a name being bestowed upon us by the Germans. For as of yet, I have not heard of anything along the lines of *"Russis", "Frankis" or "Brittis".*

Now I certainly don't want to be a *"Trotzki"* – derived from the word *"Trotz"* (defiance) and meaning something along the lines of "stubborn Steven" – but whenever a German in a conversation keeps on saying things like *"Amis"* this and *"Amis"* that, sometimes I just can't refrain from saying: "I don't fundamentally object to hearing you *"Deutschis"* use the word *'Ami'* but maybe it would be better if you *"Deutschis"* wouldn't overdo it so much." Ah, this is how to make myself popular in Germany...

Germans evidently don't give much thought to the matter when using the word *"Ami"*, but they wouldn't even consider talking about a Polish person in the same manner. Only a particularly uninhibited Swedish fellow student of mine in Göttingen dared to address one of the Polish guys directly in the following manner *"Hey, Polski?"*. None of the natives would have dared to do that. (Perhaps this phenomenon is similar to how Americans can, even nowadays, carelessly refer to Germans as "Krauts", but would no longer dare call the Japanese "Japs".)

***

In Göttingen, I attended a few courses, but my major was clearly in *"Alltagsdeutsch mit Schwerpunkt Kneipendeutsch"* („Everyday-German" with a focus on "Pub-German"), and my minors were in *"Faulenzen"* (Lounging around), *"Sightseeing"* (Sight-seeing) and *"tourimäßiges Verhalten"* (touristic behavior.)

After two and a half years of working in Chicago with lots of stress and little vacation time, I truly appreciated my newly found freedoms. My new motto was therefore: *"In der Ruhe liegt der David."* (In tranquility can be found David.) Since I now had so much time on my hands, I could be on the go just about every weekend. And while traveling in the train, not only could I admire the blossoming landscapes, but also my blossoming vocabulary lists: an unbeatable combination in my opinion.

One weekend in October, I travelled to Düsseldorf in order to visit Nicole, whom I had met several months previously in a library in Chicago, and who was now back in Germany, where she was staying with her family. Her mother was somewhat nervous about meeting me, since she did not speak English and had never been in the USA. She simply assumed that I, as an American, could probably not speak much German, if any at all. Upon my arrival in Düsseldorf, I quickly noticed that information to the contrary could not be processed by her. The consequence: simple conversations.

After Nicole had introduced us to each other, her mother pointed to her stomach (and to the bottle of ketchup that she had bought the day before on my behalf), and asked me: *"David, hast du ... Hunger?"* (David, are you .... hungry?) In the train I had crammed lots of *"Beamtendeutsch"* into my head, so my answer was the sentence which I had memorized for just such an occasion: *"Ich bedanke mich recht herzlich für die rücksichtsvolle Erkundigung Ihrerseits, aber im Zug von Hamburg nach Düsseldorf kam ich in den Genuss einer deftigen und reichhaltigen Mahlzeit."* (I thank you most heartily for the utterly considerate inquiry from your person, but in the train from Hamburg to Düsseldorf I enjoyed a quite delicious and substantial meal.) This answer nevertheless evidently sounded to her ears more along the lines of: *"Nein, ich nicht Hunger haben"* (No, I no hungry). The conversation continued along similar lines with a bottle of Coca-Cola on the topic of my thirst, and a comic-book on the topic of reading material. With a pillow in her hand, she asked me later that evening: *"David, bist du ... schläfrig?"* (David, are you ... sleepy?) while she made some snoring sounds. I had to admit that I was indeed starting to have some problems refraining from yawning. Fortunately, Nicole was there to do some interpreting for us!

I could imagine why she was somewhat at a loss in that situation, for I will never forget the first time that I, myself, met someone who did not speak my native language. In my part of the USA this was, after all, not a regular occurrence. I was 15 years old, and my mother took me along to a Mexican folk-dance performance. After the first several dances, we decided to buy a program, since we really didn't understand at all what was going on. At the sales-counter I asked a Mexican youth how much a program cost. His answer: "Five Dollars." So far, so good, I thought, but then I asked him whether he could change a twenty dollar bill. His answer: "Five Dollars." Somewhat confused, I asked him in my most friendly manner how long he had been living in the USA. Once again: "Five Dollars." Next to him behind the counter stood his pretty sister: Though the temptation was great, I could just manage to resist asking the question which popped into my head ...

In November, I then visited Anja's parents in the scenic hilly region known as the *"Ostharz"*, located in the former East Germany. The couple was also very hospitable and showed me all sorts of sights from the area. Particularly unforgettable for me was the visit to the Panorama-Museum in Bad Frankenhausen, where there was a gigantic drawing, approximately 1,700 square meters in size, by Werner Tübke depicting a scene from the German Peasants' War, which took place from 1524 to 1525. In front of the entrance stood seven flagpoles, of which only one was now in use. Atop it fluttered a solitary German flag in the wind. When I asked Anja's mother why the other six flag poles stood there unused, she explained it as follows: Though Warsaw may still exist, the Warsaw Pact, comprised of its seven friendly member states, no longer does.

The tour was conducted in German, which meant that I was fully preoccupied with the dual tasks of understanding what the tour guide was saying and yet somehow remaining inconspicuous. In an instant my efforts were all for naught, however, as Anja's mother suddenly exclaimed to the guide in German: "Could you please speak more slowly? We have a guest from the U!S!A!" I was astonished with how much power three letters could be emphasized. All eyes turned to me while I looked in vain for a place to hide.

Resolutely and without mercy, Anja's mother continued: "Our friend from the U!S!A! speaks some German, but he doesn't understand everything when it goes too fast. He comes from the far away U!S!A!, and it would be a shame if our friend from the U!S!A! would miss important some details just because he comes from the U!S!A!." I couldn't tell from the looks on the faces of the other museum visitors whether they were envious of her having such an exotic guest, or whether they perhaps would rather rebuild the Berlin Wall to keep people like me out. But one thing was clear: here in this area, people didn't get many visitors from one of the new "friendly countries".

In a souvenir shop in Chemnitz, I was reminded once again that I seemed to enjoy a certain special status in the former GDR. Without any ulterior motives, I asked the pretty, young sales-lady how the *"Räuchermännchen"* (a smoking man figurine typical in Saxony) could emit fragrant smoke from his pipe without himself going up in flames. "Where are YOU from?", she enquired. Somewhat confused, I replied quietly: "I am from the u.s.a., but where does the fragrant smoke come from?" She beamed at me: "How long have you been in Chemnitz?"

Slowly it was becoming clear to me that I was not the one who was going to be posing the questions around here: "I have been here since yesterday." Full of enthusiasm she exclaimed: "And already you can speak so much German!" Her enthusiasm struck me as unexpectedly as her next question did: "Do you have a girlfriend?" In retrospect I probably shouldn't have bought five of the *"Räuchermännchen"*. But at least her autograph and telephone number was scribbled on the receipt. That evening we met up in a *"Kneipe"*, where she explained how many similarities we had: "You are an *'Ami'* and I am a *'Zoni'!"* (The term *"Zoni"* comes from the slang expression used before the fall of the Berlin Wall for people living in the *"Zone"* or the GDR.) All of the sudden I found the term *"Ami"* not to be all that bad after all...

While on the go in the train, I caught sight of all sorts of what I considered to be funny village names, such as *"Dämligen"*, *"Oberhäslich"*, *"Verbummlingen"*, *"Wladirostock"*, *"Dummsdorf"* and *"Betudlingen"* – although I must admit that, in retrospect, I am no longer certain that they all really had exactly those names. After all, I had just discovered that people were allowed to drink *"Elefantenbier"* out of gigantic beer cans while on the train in Germany. (In the USA, of course, people aren't even allowed to drink the weakest variety of beer out of tiny cans in the trains.) Many of my fellow male travelers evidently had a strong affinity for just this type of beer consumption, and, out of solidarity, I proverbially joined the club for one particular stretch of the journey...

Now and then I was able to share my touristic existence by taking short trips with several of my fellow foreign students from the University of Göttingen. Since we knew all about the German affinity for diminutives, we referred to ourselves as the *"Ausis"* (short for the *"Ausländer"* – the foreigners – and not to be confused with the "Aussies", who come from Australia). And, thanks to the *"Schönes-Wochenende-Tickets"* (referred to us as the *"Schwotis"*), we *"Ausländer"* got to just about all over the place.

Back then, the *"Schwoti"* only cost 35 D-Mark for five people – and then we could "train around" the whole country for an entire weekend at no additional cost! During our German classes, we formed travel groups in order to ensure that we utilized the full capacity of the *"Schwoti"*. It was never particularly difficult to find a suitable travel destination, since there were so many interesting places to go to. The only complicating factor was that Hilde, who came from Holland, kept wanting to travel to Hildesheim …

For us, the *"Schwoti"* was the perfect means to get to know Germany, Germans and other foreigners – especially foreigners with big families. In the beginning, Germany may have seemed small to me, but thanks to the *"Schwoti"* the distances became enormous! (As part of the inexpensive *"Schwoti"* concept, a traveler could only use the slow regional trains which evidently made a stop at each and every one-horse-town along the tracks.) My trip from Leipzig to Göttingen of only 200 some kilometers ended up taking almost as long as a flight from Leipzig to Chicago!

One weekend, we took the train together to Berlin in order to have a look at the remains of the Berlin Wall. Hilde, however, was not satisfied by the mere sight of the remains. She wanted to truly "experience" the Berlin Wall instead. And since, of all of us, Hilde had the most courage, coupled with the smallest vocabulary, she was already on top of the Wall when she called down: *"David! Was bedeutet UNTERSAGT?"*

(David! What does *"UNTERSAGT"* mean?) Since I knew that it meant "prohibited", I responded: "It means that you have gone too far, Hilde!" Indeed, it is not always easy to read between the lines when there is only one line …

Included in our travelling group was often a young Swedish couple comprised of the pretty Sara and her boyfriend, Fredrick. As a German-Studies student, Sara loved the German language and was therefore in Göttingen. As her new boyfriend, Fredrick loved Sara and therefore was also in Göttingen. And he had come to Germany despite previously not knowing much at all about the German language. Fredrick had quickly earned our respect with dedication and persistence when it came to doing his German homework. Though every time I saw Sara flash her beautiful smile in his direction, I understood the source of so much diligence.

One evening I went with the Danish girl and the two Swedes to the movies. We wanted to watch a German movie, so we chose *"Jenseits der Stille"* (Beyond Silence) which told the story of a young woman who, against the wishes of her deaf parents, becomes a musician. As we left the movie theater, I asked Fredrick what he thought of the film. His answer: *"Der Film war sehr ausländer-freundlich."* (The movie was very foreigner-friendly.) Surprised by his statement, I said: "But there weren't even any foreigners in the entire movie!" To which Fredrick replied: "No, but the people in the movie all spoke slowly and clearly. I found that very considerate for foreigners."

I understood exactly what he meant. After all, I had been with Adelheid at the movies a few weeks prior. We watched the Jane Austen-movie "Sense and Sensibility", which in German is called *"Sinn und Sinnlichkeit"*. But I found the movie to be so difficult to understand at times that I renamed it for myself to *"Sinn und Sinnlosigkeit"* (Sense and Senselessness").

One day in December many of the other *"Ausies"* suddenly stormed the streets in wonderment. I remained inside and yawned, for the occasion was the first snowfall of the year. But the tropical *"Ausies"* were all agog. They ran around as if *"schneekrank"* (snow-sick) and were pleased as punch. Now, I also think that snow is beautiful, but for me back at home, snow had always meant a ton of extra work outside. But at least it also meant that Christmas was just around the corner.

„Supi!" (German slang for "Super!")

20: Confusing Contractions

As is mentioned relatively early on in most German grammar books, there are a bunch of abbreviations in German, just like there are in many other languages. One variety of these is the prepositional contractions. Examples of these in English include "can't" for "cannot", "I'm" for "I am", "he's" for "he is" and "we'll" for "we will" or "we shall".

Many prepositional contractions in German are relatively easy to identify, even when there is no apostrophe around to identify them as such. Examples include: *"am"* (at the), *"ans"* (at the), *"aufs"* (on the), *"beim"* (at the), *"im"* (in the), *"ins"* (into the), *"vom"* (of the), *"zum"* (to the), *"zur"* (to the), and so on. These examples of contractions are usually among those mentioned in grammar books since they belong to the "well-behaved" category. In fact, not only can they almost always be used, but in many cases they even must be used. At least if one doesn't want to sound somewhat dim-witted to German ears.

For instance, even though they are all grammatically correct, the following sentences spoken by a man to a woman would sound worse than stiff to her: *"Ich kenne dich irgendwie **von dem** Sehen her. Vielleicht war es **in einem** Kino, warst du neulich **in dem** Abaton? Ich glaube, es war **bei dem** Warten **an dem** Ausgang, als wir **in das** Gespräch kamen. **An dem** Besten gibst du mir deine Telefonnummer."* (I know you from somewhere. Perhaps it was in a movie theater. Were you recently at the Abaton? I believe it was while we were waiting at the exit when we started a conversation. It would be best if you gave me your telephone number.) After such a start, I'm afraid that the man is not going to be getting much information from her at all...

On the other hand, there are also numerous prepositional contractions which are given the cold shoulder by German grammar books. As a result, it takes a lot longer for a non-native German speaker to figure out how to use these correctly. Many of these contractions might be alright for informal conversation, but they should best be avoided in official written communications. On a daily basis, I hear colleagues say things like: that they have driven their car "before the weekend in front of the building" *("vorm Wochenende vors Gebäude")*, but should I dare to write in a German financial statement audit report that the client will go "before the end of the audit to court" *(„vorm Prüfungsabschluss vors Gericht")*, then my sentence would surely not survive the bright red correcting-pencils of the German typing-pool ladies.

Moreover, one can write that a matter *"ins Geld geht"* (is serious money), but not that it *"ums Geld geht"* (is a matter of money). In the news one could read that in a fire twenty people *"ums Leben kamen"* (died), but not that twenty corpses *"ums Gebäude lagen"* (laid around a building).

Another variety of the German abbreviations is treated even more shabbily in German grammar books, even though this sort abounds in the everyday spoken language. These black sheep are the so-called "swallowed syllables". The power of the swallowed syllable were demonstrated to me by my younger brother Joe when he once asked me: "David, was does *"nen heben"* mean?" He was very diligently learning German, and I felt like a good, wiser, older brother, as I could normally quickly answer most of his many questions regarding the German language. But this question stumped me.

I asked him for some context regarding the question. (This is not just a good way to stall for time when trying to come up with an answer. Many words are indeed impossible to translate accurately without their context.) Joe complied and replied: "David, *zuerst packt man seine sieben Sachen in den Flieger rein. Dann geht man raus aus dem Regen, der Sonne entgegen."* He continued: "So far, so good, as I know that this means: first you pack all your stuff into the plane before you can flee the rainy weather to head south for the sunshine, but before you can experience the bikinis, as the songs says, you have to *'nen heben'.*" Then I finally realized what the answer was: it was a contraction of *"einen heben"* (to raise one (alcoholic drink).) It was also suddenly clear to me that he had been trying to memorize the lyrics of the cool German song *"Ab in den Süden"* (Off to the South).

I myself had had a similar experience with a friend of Adelheid's by the name of Christoph when we were strolling about town once. He and I got along really well, since we seemed to have similar senses of humor. But, unfortunately, I did not always understand what exactly Christoph was talking about, since he – like many teenagers the world over – didn't have a very clear pronunciation when he spoke. As a result, for a time I mistakenly thought that an amazing number of girls in that small city had the same name.

This misconception was essentially due to the fact that, whenever we were walking around together without Adelheid, Christoph repeatedly pointed out girls whom we spied from a distance on the street and described them as follows: *"Siehst du die Frau da? Das ist 'ne Nette. Und die da drüben, das ist auch 'ne Nette."* (Do you see the girl over there? That is *'ne Nette'*. And that one over there, that is also *'ne Nette'*. – In German, the phrase *"eine Nette"* is an abbreviation for "a nice looking woman".) Not until I asked him why so many women were named *"Nanette"* did he realize that I wasn't exactly comprehending the gist of what he had been trying to tell me.

***

Not only linguistic short-cuts can be dangerous for a relationship: the same holds true for mini-vacations. I came to this realization when I took a vacation that year shortly after spending Christmas with Adelheid. Our trip was a brief excursion to Paris. In spite of her noble birth, Adelheid was by no means a lady of luxury. Flying was out of the question, especially since there weren't any low-budget airlines around back then yet. We therefore took an overnight bus directly after Christmas from Hannover to Paris. Unfortunately, on the day of our departure a snowstorm hit which threw the entire endeavor into chaos. While waiting outside in line for our bus, which was having a tough time getting any traction on the snow and ice, I silently made a wish for our very own sleigh and group of magical flying reindeer.

After we had survived the artic wait outside and then the ensuing battle for seats within the warm bus, we tried first to thaw off and then to get some sleep during the trip. Slowly drifting off, I wondered if Napoleon had experienced similarly uncomfortable feelings during his icily uncomfortable journey from the snows of the wild east back to Paris in 1812 after his failed expedition to subdue Russia. Fortunately, a welcoming committee was waiting for us in Paris. This consisted of our favorite two "Göttingen guys", Jerome and Juri. Since Jerome came from Paris and was a friendly Frenchman, he had invited us all to stay with him.

At the end of December 1996, it was bitterly cold all over in Western Europe. According to the weather reports, it was the coldest winter in decades. Since Juri and I were well acquainted with continental climates, we had enough respect for the power of winter weather: Juri wore his Russian fur-hat and I wore my woolly American ear-muffs. Fashion conscious as she was, Adelheid was not at all amused by my attire. In fact, she refused to be seen within a radius of ten meters from me as long as I was wearing my "crazy Mickey-Mouse-ears". She also did not laugh when I asked her if she thought that I was what the Germans refer to as a *"Schicki-Micky"* (loosely translated: "Trendy-Travis").

As was befitting a Frenchman of style, Jerome also only wore a thin chic jacket without any covering for his head. While we were walking about, I constantly wondered how he could endure such cold in such style. I felt certain that, were I in his place, my ears would quickly have frozen off. But Jerome and Adelheid evidently both lived life by the same motto: When one is out and about, it is better to look good than to feel good.

I think that the only thing that displeased Adelheid more than my winter fashion sense was my habit of taking so many photos. After each click of my camera, she would simply shake her head and sigh: "Only the Japanese are worse..."

On the third day of our vacation, Juri and I had to fend for ourselves alone in Paris, since Jerome and Adelheid were both lying in their respective beds with high fevers back at Jerome's parents' house. When we had gotten up out of bed, I was tempted to tease Adelheid by telling her that I had "told her so", but her stern countenance informed me that such a course of action would not be at all good for my own state of health. In fact, one glance from her was all she needed to make unmistakably clear that, should I try, I wouldn't be needing any earmuffs to keep my ears warm for a long time.

Now on our own, we were really a terrific trio: a Russian, an American and the German language. Not only did we explore the streets of Paris, but also the paths of our only mutual lingo. Juri impressed me once again with his collection of puns, which he seemed to be able to conjure out of his fur-covered sleeves at the drop of a fur-covered hat. Fortunately, Adelheid was not around, since she probably would not have been at all amused. Though almost impossible to translate without losing their charm, here are a few of his German language gems:

- *"Wie teuer ist die Sojawurst im Bioladen?"* *"Schweineteuer."*
- *"Was braucht man für manche Sitzungen?"* *"Viel Stehvermögen."*
- *"Wie wirkt man, wenn man Lampenfieber hat?"* *"Etwas unterbelichtet."*

(Here the loose English translations:)
- "How expensive is the Soja-sausage at the organic foods store?" "Pig-expensive."
- "What does one need for some business sittings?" "A good standing in staying power."
- "How does stage-fright caused by bright lights make one look?" "Somewhat dim."

But when Juri confessed, *"David, gestern war ich nach dem langen Tag völlig k.o."*, (David, after the long day yesterday, I was really *"k.o."*) I recognized at last my chance to finally be able to make my own little linguistic contribution to the conversation. Since Juri didn't speak any English, I was certain that he – along with many Germans – did not know that the abbreviation *"k.o."* comes from the English boxing expression "knocked out". But when I asked him if he knew the source of the term *"k.o."*, Juri replied confidently: "But of course! It is the opposite of "o.k."!"

But he was actually of the opinion that Germans should say *"a.k."* instead of *"o.k."*, as this would stand for *"alles klar"* (everything's clear). If it were truly up to him, the expression *"i.O."* would be even better, as this stood for *"in Ordnung"* (in order). After all, if there is one thing that Germans appreciate, then it is order. But there I had to contradict Juri, for should one say *"i.O."* (pronounced "ee oh") two or three times quickly in a row, then one might run the danger of sounding like a donkey.

In spite of our lack of knowledge regarding the local terrain and language, we succeeded in ascending the Eiffel Tower. Once we made it to the top, we were confronted with yet another problem: Where were the restrooms? And since Juri didn't speak any English, it was up to me to play the translator in our little group. Unfortunately, none of the natives seemed either willing or able to speak English. Time and time again, it was the same old story:

Me: *"Parlez-vous anglais?"*

Native: *"Non."*

Me: *"Parlez-vous allemand?"*

Native: *"Non!"*

Me: *"Parlez-vous russe?"*

Native: *"Non?"*

After a while, I finally lost patience: I wanted to finally get a positive answer for a change! Therefore I reached into the very depths of my memory in order to summon all my French language powers. I asked the very next man who walked by *"Pardonnez moi, Monsieur. Parlez-vous français?"* Finally my ears heard the sweet sounds of a *"Mais oui!"*. This pleased me greatly for a few seconds, at least until I realized that this answer didn't really solve our core problem at that moment.

There, on top of the Eiffel tower, I was overcome by the feeling of how symbolic our situation truly was: An American and a Russian together in the heart of Paris peacefully chatting away. A mere few years previously and that would have been almost unimaginable for me. And the fact that we were speaking in German gave our constellation a particularly special touch – something that the two German tourists next to us evidently also thought as they stared at us, all astonishment.

Soon thereafter, not only our vacation in Paris, but also my time as Adelheid's boyfriend came to a sudden end. At the bus-stop in Hannover she said to me as we parted: *"Tja, David,* *man **sieht** sich!"* (David, we will see each other around.) Unfortunately, I misunderstood this as: *"Tja, David, man **siezt** sich!"* (David, we now should use the formal form of the word "you" when talking to each other.) So once I started using this *"Sie"* formal form on Adelheid, she was all the more certain that we weren't meant for each other.

At the beginning of January I needed to revise my plans regarding my further stay in Germany, as two things were becoming clear to me: First of all, a *"Hauptstudium"* (loosely translated: "Master's degree") in Germany can take a really long time. Secondly, I was really broke. It doesn't matter how many cuts in expenditures one makes, if one doesn't have any income, sooner or later, the money is going to run out. I needed to find some sort of income if I was going to be able to stay in the country.

Slowly things were starting to get a little uneasy for me in my life of ease. I would need to find a job quickly to foot the bills if I ever wanted to gain a firm foothold in the land of my forefathers …

21: How do you "du"?

Where modern English just has one word at its disposal: "you", in German one has to choose between the seven alternatives of *"du"*, *"dich"*, *"dir"*, *"ihr"*, *"euch"*, *"Sie"* and *"Ihnen"*. As a result, most native English speakers learning German sooner or later wonder aloud: "How do you '*du*?"

Which of the various German "you" forms is correct depends upon many factors. The relatively harmless factors are the objective ones, such as: how many "yous" are there? And in which grammatical case are they at the moment? Unfortunately, the determination of the correct "you" form is also dependent upon a variety of subjective factors. These tend to be somewhat harder to pin down. First of all, how well does one know the "you" in question? Secondly, how well would one like to know the "you"? And thirdly, how well would this "you" like to get to know you?

Fortunately, there are some basic rules which can help in the decision making process, such as the age, the profession and the vanity of the "you" in question. One must also take into the consideration the situation in which one encounters the "you". If one meets a young *"Fräulein"* in the disco, one should use the informal *"du"* form, unless ones happen to be the bouncer at the door. If one, however, meets the same *"Fräulein"* at the reception desk of a company at which one is applying for a job, then one had better use the formal *"Sie"* form, if one would like to ever see her again.

An additional helpful ground-rule is as follows: If one would use the last name, then one should probably use the formal *"Sie"* form. In this manner, one is actually erring on the side of caution.

Over the years, I have gained the following impression: the further one journeys northwards in the linguistic territory of the Germanic peoples, the more dominant the *"du"* form becomes. In the flat lands of northern Germany one tends to quickly switch over to *"du"*-ing. And in the Scandinavian languages such as Swedish, almost everyone uses the informal *"du"* form. (By the way, *"du"* translated into Swedish, Norwegian and Danish is simply *"du"*, in contrast to the extremely complicated Finnish, where it is probably something along the lines of *"duiiiikökökii"*.) An exception in Sweden would perhaps be an encounter with the Swedish king himself, but then only if the subject feels like it. On the other hand, in southern Germany, Austria and Switzerland, people tend to stick with the formal *"Sie"* form much longer. Indeed, if they ever switch to *"du*-ing" before they depart for the afterlife.

Despite the many difficulties in choosing the correct German "you", it is very important to make the right choice. Of the seven possibilities mentioned above, not a single one lets itself be treated like a dwarf. Choosing the wrong "you" can have far reaching consequences – some of which may be funny, but others can jeopardize one's career. In the beginning of my internship in Hamburg, for instance, I simply assumed that I should say *"Sie"* to all of the "important" people, such as the Managers and Partners, whereas I should say *"du"* to the "less important" people, such as the secretaries. This was definitely a big mistake on my part. Some of the Managers and Partners did actually want to stay on *"Sie"* terms with me, but many of them were pleased by my politeness and then proposed that we say *"du"* to each other. None of the secretaries smiled, however. It quickly became clear to me that most of the secretaries not only wanted to stay on *"Sie"* terms with me, but also that they are very important persons...

To my own astonishment, after a while I actually began to really appreciate this variety of choice in the German language. For example, whenever in public one overhears a man and a woman arguing. If they are using the *"du"* form, then it is fairly clear that the couple is probably just bickering over something trivial. However, should they be exchanging harsh words using the *"Sie"* form, then it is more likely to be a serious situation, into which a gentlemen ought perhaps to intervene.

After hanging out for several years with the German language, sometimes it feels strange for me when I speak English with an important person, and I then realize that I only have the "you" form at my disposal. Somehow this now gives me the awkward feeling that I am, in some way, invading his or her personal space.

***

While I sat in the large chambers of the head of the Hamburg office in January 1997, with the "Big Cheese" himself sitting across his desk from me, one thing was crystal clear to me: I should not say *"du"* to this man. After a brief discussion, he sprang into action and grabbed the telephone receiver. What he said to the person on the other end of the telephone line sounded very promising to me: *"Wissen Sie, ob Herr Bergmann morgen etwas bei der großen Tochter machen könnte?"* (Do you know if there is anything that Mr. Bergmann could do at the ‚big daughter' tomorrow?" (I had not yet learned that *"große Tochter"* could mean not only "big daughter" but also "large subsidiary"…) Evidently he got a positive answer, for he then hung up the receiver and handed me a piece of paper with the address of a client written on it, saying to me: "Herr Bergmann, that is where you are going to start to audit here in Germany."

I had been working in Hamburg at a *"Wirtschaftsprüfungsgesellschaft"* (Public Accounting Firm) for one entire day. After a semester in Göttingen, I had gotten the misconception that I had more or less mastered the German language in the meantime. Then came my first week of work and my estimation of my abilities was severely revised downwards. I was namely no longer among students from all parts of the globe, but rather in the world of *"Büro-Deutsch"* (Office German). I now found myself in the world of German Auditing, where thoughts are not only seldom free, but actually usually rather expensive.

The *"Prüfungsleiter"* (audit supervisor) at the large subsidiary was named Ulf, and he was happy to have me, at least in the beginning. Already my first assignment was a bit too much for me:

"David, prüf mal die PRAP." („David, audit the ‚PRAP'.")

"Was ist ein PRAP?" („What is a ‚PRAP'?")

"Das ist wie ein ARAP, nur umgekehrt." („It is like a ‚ARAP', just reversed.")

Luckily for me I was quickly able to find the Audit Report from the previous year which contained explanations for many of the abbreviations and contractions. I was thereby able to ascertain that an *"ARAP"* is actually an *"aktiver Rechnungs-abgrenzungsposten"* (prepaid expense). And not, as I had originally suspected, someone who lives in the deserts of the Middle East.

Fortunately, before my first day at work I had read an article in a business magazine about how one should behave in the German business world when one is completely clueless, (or as the Germans say *"von jeglicher Ahnung unbeleckt"*): One simply does not admit it. One never should say for instance: *"Ich verstehe gar nichts!"* (I don't understand anything!) Instead, one should camouflage one's lack of knowledge by stating: *"Ich fühle mich zurzeit nicht in der Lage, dieses Thema abschließend beurteilen zu können."* (I consider myself currently not in the position of being able to conclusively form a judgment on the matter.)

Further examples of wrong and right answers in difficult situations:

1. *"Ich habe es vergessen."* – *"Das ist mir entfallen."*
2. *"Geht mich das was an?"* – *"Das tangiert mich nur peripher."*
3. *"Ich bin nicht mehr sicher."* – *"Wenn ich mich recht entsinne."*
4. *"Da blicke ich nicht durch."* – *"Das geht über meinen Horizont."*
5. *"Ich denke schon."* – *"Nach menschlichem Ermessen."*
6. *"Ich fand es nirgendwo heraus."* – *"Es ließ sich nicht eruieren."*
7. *"Weil mich das nervte."* – *"Aus gegebenem Anlass."*
8. *"Ich habe keine Lust."* – *"Dies liegt nicht in meinem Aufgabenbereich."*
9. *"Ich weiß es gar nicht."* – *"Weiß der Kuckuck (bzw. Henker, Teufel oder Geier)."*

(Here are the approximate English translations:)

1. "I've forgotten." – "It must have slipped my mind."
2. "Why should I care?" – "That only concerns me peripherally."
3. "I'm not sure anymore." – "If I recall correctly."
4. "I don't get it." – "That is beyond me."
5. "I think so." – "According to human reasoning."
6. "I couldn't find out." – "The information could not be elicited."
7. "Because it annoyed me." – "Due to recent occurrences."
8. "I don't want to." – "That is not in my area of responsibility."
9. "I don't know." – "Only the cuckoo bird knows (or the executioner, devil or vulture)."

In the beginning, I was deeply impressed by everything that the cuckoo bird and co. seemed to know. My favorite among all of these pithy phrases is however: *"Das entzieht sich meiner Kenntnis."* (The answer eludes me.) For in this manner one hints that one can't help being clueless.

The consequences that Wolfgang drew when he once was forced to admit that he did not, in fact, know the answer to a question seemed rather brutal to me: *"David, dann ist anzuwenden... im HGB Paragraph ... uh, was weiß ich? Uh, 265 im Absatz ... Schieß mich tot!"* (David, then we have to apply... in HGB Paragraph ... uh, what do I know? Uh, 265 in sentence... Shoot me dead!) Why I should shoot Wolfgang dead, just because he didn't know the answer by heart, was something that I did not know at that moment. But I reckoned that the cuckoo bird definitely must know the answer!

At the end of each audit, the Audit-Manager stopped on by to see how the engagement was progressing. The Manager at my first client was named Klaus. Among other things he took a long close look at our working papers. This seemed to make my colleague Wolfgang rather nervous – I believe he was suffering from a sort of "Klaus-trophobia".

After a few weeks in Hamburg, I began to miss the times when I was still among all of those students back in Göttingen. So I resolved to check out the university campus in Hamburg. Once there, I spied a sign from the international Student organization "Aiesec" which gave me a sudden warm and fuzzy feeling. In Göttingen I had been a member of Aiesec, and it was thanks to that group that I made it to Hamburg. Perhaps some background information here would be helpful...

In the beginning of January 1997, Aiesec had organized a so-called *"Firmenkontaktveranstaltung"* (Companies on Campus event) with which I helped out. During the planning session I recognized a chance to escape my current cashless-

predicament by placing my name up top on the list of students who would be having interviews with one of the "Big 5" public-accounting-firms.

Contrary to my own expectations, my interview went brilliantly. The senior manager who interrogated me, "Herr Dr. Z.", gave me the impression that I actually had a few advantages compared with the other applicants. After all, among other things, I had a university degree, some work experience and a native language that is worth something in Germany. And fortunately for me, he did not pose any complicated business questions. For instance, if I could translate the German concept of the *"ewige Rente"* into English. Had he asked, I surely would have given the wrong answer of: "What a person gets when they retire in Germany at the age of 55 years". (Correct would be "perpetuity for valuations".)

At the end of the interview, Herr Dr. Z. concluded by asking me: "Herr Bergmann, do you know Hamburg?" I thought to myself: "Hm … there is a harbor and the Reeperbahn. I suppose that it can't be all that bad." This is not what I said to him, though. Instead, I exclaimed: "But of course! It is the most beautiful city in all of Germany!" Judging by his smile, I realized that I had probably chosen the right answer. Summoning my courage, I then asked him: "Could I perhaps have, in the summer maybe, a modest little internship?", Deep inside, I expected an answer somewhat along the lines of "Don't call us. We won't call you either." I was therefore all the more surprised by his reply: "Herr Bergmann, could you start with us next Monday?"

And thus my studies in Göttingen ended much more quickly than I had expected. When I told Frau Wilbärt about this development that evening, large tears welled up in her eyes. To me, these definitely did not look like tears of sadness.

Even more surprising for me than the job offer itself was

the notification three months later that I had survived the internship and that the company was prepared to make me an offer for a full-time position. This came as somewhat of a surprise to me, for it meant that I would be getting paid a normal salary while I continued my "learning by *'du'*-ing".

PS. One of the more colorful words in the English language is the word "doozie", which is pronounced just like the combination of the two main German you-forms *"du-Sie"*. It means something that is extraordinary, often in the context of troublesome, difficult or problematic. I doubt that this can be a coincidence...

22: Rolling with the German R's

The main problem for native English speakers when it comes to pronouncing German is the letter R. (This statement probably doesn't come as a surprise to any Germans...) I once read in a travel guide for Germany that there are three types of high-schools in the country (*"Gymnasium", "Realschule" and "Hauptschule"*), and that there aren't drinking fountains in any of them – in contrast to American high-schools. It is a somewhat similar situation when it comes to the German R-sound: There are three possibilities of pronouncing the R, and none of them is quite like the American way.

These three options are as follows:

1. Vibrating the tip of the tongue in the front of the mouth (*"apical"*), as is typical in Switzerland.

2. Vibrating the tongue near its base (*"uvular"*), as is customary in northern Germany.

3. The simple omitting of any sound (*"Faulenzia vulgaris extremica"*), as is common almost everywhere in Germany.

Actually, the third variation is never explicitly mentioned, just as the R in German is sometimes not explicitly pronounced. To my ears, sometimes the German R is truly imperceptible, especially in northern Germany. In American English the R sound is not at all shy, and seems to go almost out of its way to attract attention. In contrast, in German sometimes I just don't hear any R and therefore have to guess whether it is even there. And I am not the only one with this problem. The little daughter of a friend of mine also had a tough time mastering the R-sound. Once she got a bad grade on her school homework, because she had spelled the German word *"Bär"* (bear) like it is pronounced: "Bea".

Misunderstandings are therefore bound to happen. For

instance, once while I was listening to a German radio station, I thought that the DJ was announcing a song by a new rock group by the name of "The Ks". Not until the songs began did I realize that he was talking about "The Cars". (In German, the word "Car" is pronounced with even less "r" than President J.F.K. would have used: "Cah".)

But especially embarrassing for me have been the situations where I falsely assumed that an R must be present. For instance, for a long while I mistakenly thought that:

- Leipzig is a *"Messerstadt"* (knife city) instead of a *"Messestadt"* (convention city).
- Old cars have their *"Türken"* (Turks) instead of their *"Tücken"* (quirks).
- In church, something can be as certain as *"die Armen"* (the poor) instead of *"das Amen"* (Amen).
- At an Italian restaurant, one buys *"Pasta Mister"* instead of *"Pasta Mista"*.
- After studying Biology, one gets a job in the *"Farmer-Industrie"* instead of the *"Pharma-Industrie"*.
- People buy ice-cream at an *"Eis-Dealer"* (ice cream dealer) instead of at an *"Eisdiele"* (Ice cream bar.)

But at least I could take some comfort in my ability, as a native English speaker, to always hear the difference between the "L" and the "R" German. This is in contrast to many Asians, who, for instance often don't hear whether a German is *"ausgelastet"* (busy) or *"ausgerastet"* (flipped out).

I remember my first pronunciation class with Frau Güllicher at the Goethe-Institut in Chicago, where we discussed just this very topic. After the class, she asked me with a concerned expression how I was doing, because I looked so worn out. I wanted to reply: *"Ich trauere furchtbar"* (I am suffering severely), but I just couldn't get the words out. No matter what Frau

Güllicher attempted in the following months, or how hard I tried, by the bitter end of my time at the Goethe-Institut I still was not able to pronounce the *"Uvular-r"* correctly. My *"Apikal-r"* wasn't so bad, but Frau Güllicher was not satisfied with this, since she came from the northern German city of Lübeck where the natives think it odd when Americans speak German using this so-called "Spanish R".

Germans seem to enjoy making fun of the problems that many Americans have in making the German R-sound. Especially annoying about this is that many Germans don't have any problems with the pronunciation of the English R-sound, primarily because they have been working on it since their childhood. As a result, it can be demoralizing for a native English speaker when a German imitates his pronunciation. I was therefore especially relieved when I noticed that most native German speakers can pronounce either the *"Apikal-r"* or the *"Uvular-r"*, but not both. In the German speaking countries, the pronunciation of the R fortunately doesn't alter the meaning of a word, but in other foreign languages it can be decisive. For instance, in Spanish *"perro"* (with a trilled-r) means "dog", whereas *"pero"* (with little tongue-rolling) means "but". Should one therefore not be able to pronounce the Spanish *"Apikal-r"*, then one can quickly go to the dogs...

In Göttingen there was even a course for people who had problems in getting rolling with the R-sound. For my first "R-Course" I was overly punctual. After eternally long stretching and relaxation exercises, we started talking some R. To my disappointment, I noticed that we were not being taught the *"Uvular-r"* which is so very important for fitting in in Northern Germany, but rather the Spanish *"Apikal-r"*. I could already do that, and in order to prove it, I let loose my very best *"perro"*. Thereupon I quickly realized that the other course participants already mastered the *"Uvular-r"* which I was trying so desperately to learn. After a few moments of mutual admiration and envy, I trudged home despondently...

After trying out all sorts of R-exercises over the years, I finally have almost learned to correctly pronounce the *"Uvular-r"*. And yet not quite completely, so I will probably always stick out in Germany. But at least no one will ever be able to claim that I haven't rrrrrrreally trrrrrrried harrrrrrrrrd.

***

During my first months at work in Hamburg several of my colleagues parted ways with the company. Evidently they had not been trying hard enough. This made me feel slightly uneasy, especially considering that I was still in the middle of my six-month probationary period.

I noticed that often when an employee left the company, the colleagues threw an *"Abschiedsparty"* (going away party). I found this concept to be a splendid idea. In any event, it was much better than the party thrown for foreigners in Germany who did not have the right residency permit. Then there was usually a *"Abschiebungsparty"* ("go away party"). It is therefore extremely important to have the appropriate *"Duldung"* (toleration), *"Billigung"* (approbation), *"Genehmigung"* (approval), *"Erlaubnis"* (permit) or *"Berechtigung"* (right) for residing in the Federal Republic of Germany. Understanding the set of laws behind these scary sounding names can be rather time-consuming. But time is something that one has in abundance when standing in the waiting-line in front of the *"Ausländeramt"* (foreigners' office) in Hamburg.

It doesn't matter where one comes from, the memories of the waiting-line at the *"Ausländeramt"* bind the peoples of all nations together. Whenever two foreigners in Hamburg meet, the conversations always begin the same. The first question is

"Wie heißt du?" (What is your name?), then *"Woher kommst du?"* (Where are you from?) and then *"Was für einen Aufenthaltsstatus hast du?"* (What kind of residency status do you have?) and finally: *"Wie viele Stunden hast du dieses Jahr in der Ausländeramtswarteschlange verbringen müssen?"* (How many hours did you have to wait this year in line at the foreigners' office?) There one could easily get the wrong impression that the German word *"Warteschlange"* (waiting line) comes from the phrase *"warteschonlange"* (waiting a long time).

Therefore my astonishment knew no bounds when I met a newly arrived Russian immigrant at a party who replied to my last question with the answer: "None." Logically, my next question was: "Whaaat?" He continued: "I am what the Germans call an *"Aussiedler"*, which is a person of German descent who has returned to the Fatherland generations after my ancestors had departed. This has all sorts of advantages: I have gotten a German passport without having to give up my original passport. I can vote here. I am not even referred to here legally as a foreigner." But then I thought to myself. Wait a moment! I can do that too. After all, my last name is as German as names come!"

On account of my German name, people in Germany don't realize at first that I am not a German. At least until I open my mouth and thereby blow my cover. When among strangers, I sometime appreciate this camouflage and keep silent for a while in order to enjoy a certain inconspicuousness for a change.

"Woher kommst du?" (Where are you from?) is a question which has been posed to me very often in Germany. The first time I heard it, I answered proudly: "I come from the USA!", since I did not expect that people could place my background so easily on account of my accent. My pride disappeared in the

blink of an eye when the follow-up question came, "That is obvious enough, but where are you from exactly?" I then decided to always answer: "Chicago". Even though I grew up almost literally among the ponies in a one-horse-town in Ohio, I subsequently lived in Chicago for several years and I know my way around there better than in any other American city. So when a German student at a college party in Hamburg asked me where I come from, I replied "Chicago". It took almost an hour before we realized that she had lived for a year in the house next to my grandparents in Ohio. Since then I usually answer: "Where I come from depends on how well you know your way around in the USA." When someone responds that their knowledge of the USA is limited to having seen a map a while back, then I still come from Chicago.

Time and time again people tell me that I have a German last name. I know that they mean well, but now I can imagine how 7-foot tall people must feel when others keep telling them how tall they are. They already are well aware of their height. As such, when I was shopping for eye-glasses once at an optician, and the sales lady was named "Frau Deutsch", of course I just couldn't refrain from telling her: *Sie haben ja einen sehr deutschen Nachnamen!"* (You have a very German last name!) Understandably, she was not overly amused...

I am often asked by Germans why I don't have a "real" American last name. Of course, there is no such thing as "real" American last names, since the USA is truly a country of immigrants from all over the world. Every name there is really real.

Unfortunately, my German last name doesn't help me out much when I am spending my free time in the "free and hanseatic Ausländeramt waiting line". Almost twenty years after I had learned that my ancestors had not actually come to the New World on the sailing ship "Mayflower", I began to do some intensive family-tree research. All sorts of interesting findings came to light: For instance, I discovered that all of my ancestors had German last names. Some of these I found to be similarly cool to *"Bergmann"*, which translates either as "mountain man" or "miner". Some of the names were *"Kaiser"* (emperor), *"Rabe"* (raven) and *"Vogelsang"* (birdsong). But there were unfortunately also a few somewhat less attractive names, such as *"Böse"* (evil), *"Stein"* (stone) and *"Deppen"* (fools).

My research revealed, moreover, that in the 1830's and 1840's all 32 of my great-great-great-grandparents emigrated from Germany to the USA, most of whom via the harbor city of Bremerhaven. I hoped that this finding would increase my chances for obtaining *"Aussiedler-Status"* in Germany. Then I would no longer need the appropriate *"Duldung"*, *"Billigung"*, *"Genehmigung"*, *"Erlaubnis"* or *"Berechtigung"*. Full of hope, I sought out the responsible *"Beamte"* (civil servent) at the *"Ausländeramt"* – and promptly received a rejection. Summarized briefly, his reasoning was: "Documents, schmocuments: *'Amis'* can't be *'Aussiedler*!"

Evidently, an *"Aussiedler"* could only be someone whose German ancestors had settled in the "The Wild East". My ancestors, on the other hand, had settled in the "Wild West" across the Atlantic Ocean. Stung by his curt rejection, I muttered to myself: "So much for the idea of 'blood principle' in Germany!"

The not-so-civil civil servant was not open to my arguments. He said: "To put it bluntly: In order to be acknowledged as an *'Aussiedler'* in the German *'Wohlfahrtsstaat'* (welfare state), one has to come from a *'Talfahrtsstaat'* (woeful state)."

I thought to myself that if I couldn't be an *"Aussiedler"*, then at least I could refer to myself as a *"Gastarbeiter"* (guest worker). After all, I was a guest in Germany, and I worked too. I explained this idea to my favorite civil servant. His answer indicated more than a slight annoyance: *"Nein,* Herr Bergmann! You are not a *"Gastarbeiter"!* Those are the workers invited from poor countries to work for a time in our factories. You are a foreigner who is YET permitted to live and work here." I didn't ask him any further questions. Otherwise he might have downgraded my *"Aufenthaltserlaubnis"* to a *"Aufenthalts-duldung".*

Even though I was disappointed, I really couldn't complain about my ancestors' sense of orientation. After all, they had obtained the right to vote, among many other civil liberties, several decades earlier than the *"Aussiedler"* from Germany who had emigrated eastwards towards the plains of Russia. These considerations cheered me up a bit the next time I stood in the waiting-line at the *"Ausländeramt",* waiting impatiently for it to get rolling …

23: "Doinglish"

It is generally not a good idea to laugh all too loudly during an important business meeting, especially when the CEO is talking about a serious subject matter. However, for once I was actually innocent: For if the CEO had just spoken standard German, then I surely wouldn't have made such a spectacle of myself. But rather than simply informing us in an appropriate tone that the company was going to have to dismiss some workers, he instead said: *"Ein paar 'Peoplechen' müssen 'rausgekickt' werden."* (loosely translated: "We're going to have to give a few 'little people' a 'big boot' in the butt.") I just couldn't suppress my mirth.

Admittedly, very rarely do quotes from German soccer players pop into my head, but in that moment I could not help but think of Andreas Möller, who once said *"vom Feeling her habe ich ein schlechtes Gefühl"* ("I feel like I have a bad feeling about this.") And in this case, I did indeed have an uneasy feeling in my gut. This is something I often get whenever a German is speaking in the "language of poets and philosophers" and then suddenly avails himself of an English term, regardless of whether there is already an adequate (or yet even better) German word for whatever it is he wants to say.

It seems that more and more English words are now being used in the German language. This phenomenon has many names, from *"Neudeutsch"* (new German), to *"Germisch"* (German-English) or *"Denglish"* (Deutsch-English). However, I find these designations much too positive for such a linguistic mish-mash, and therefore I plead for something more fittingly funny-sounding: *"Doinglish"* (Deutsch-English).

Things can get particularly bizarre in the magazine landscape. For instance, I recently read in the German magazine *Der Spiegel* the following headline for the cover story:

"Albert Speer: Manager des Bösen" (Albert Speer: Manager of Evil). What an anachronism for Germany's supposedly very serious news magazine! Now I'm looking forward to the following cover stories:

- *"Jesus Christus: Sunny Boy der Welt"* – ("Jesus Christ: Sunny Boy of the World")
- *"Dschingis Khan: Killer der Steppe"* – ("Genghis Khan: Killer of the Steppes")
- *"Mozart: Singer-Songwriter der Alpen"* – ("Mozart: Singer-Songwriter of the Alps)
- *"Napoleon: Globalplayer der Franzosen"* – ("Napoleon: Global-Player of the French").

When Germans get together to discuss something why is this no longer called *"eine Besprechung"* (meeting), but rather *"ein Meeting"*? And who needs the word 'meeting' anyway when the following words are already readily available: *"Konferenz"* (conference), *"Diskussion"* (discussion), *"Treffen"* (get-together), *"Tagung"* (meeting), *"Sitzung"* (meeting) and *"Besprechung"* (meeting). The only thing that's missing is if Germans would get together in the evening in order to have a *"Speaking"* instead of *"Klatsch und Tratsch"* (gossip session), *"Klönschnack"* (chatting session), *"Plaudern"* (chit-chat session) or *"Schwatzen"* (gabbing session).

I often enter a room at work or at a party where I am the only non-native German speaker present. I therefore find it somewhat ironic that so often the natives greet me with a proclamation of: *"Jetzt kommt der Native-speaker!"* ("Here comes the native speaker!").

In order to keep abreast of the adoption of so many English words into German, I have read several books on this topic. My findings: some people seem to find the development of *"Doinglish"* to be fascinating, others think it is annoying, some consider it appalling and others think it's just plain funny. I find it to be all of these things.

It is fascinating, for example, when you take a look at how the meanings of some English words in used in German have developed over the course of time. One good example is the rapid ascent of the English word "job". During my language course in Göttingen in 1996, my German teacher Frau Tamchina sternly corrected me when I referred to my prior position at an accounting firm in Chicago as *"mein Job"*. "Mr. Bergmann, in German, a "job" is only something temporary or for a little extra income!" Nowadays, however, even the German Chancellor talks about his "job".

Frau Tamchina probably goes crazy whenever her work colleagues no longer use German sentences such as *"Seitdem ich meinen **Teilzeitarbeitsplatz** bei McDonald's aufgegeben habe und diese **Vollzeitstelle** hier habe, ist es nicht mehr meine **Aufgabe** zu überprüfen, ob der Drucker seine **Aufträge** durchführt."* (Since I quit my **part-time position** at McDonald's and have begun my **full-time career** here, it is no longer my **task** to make sure that the printer **is printing** as programmed." Instead they say: *"Seitdem ich meinen **Job** bei McDonald's aufgegeben habe und diesen **Job** hier habe, ist es nicht mehr mein **Job** zu schauen, ob der Drucker seine **Jobs** durchführt."* (Since I quit my **job** at McDonald's and got this **job**, it's no longer my **job** to make sure the printer is doing its **job** right.)

And it's not just that English words are becoming more and more common in German, but even German words are being used more and more in the "English-Style". These have snuck into everyday conversation via the dubbing of English language movies and TV programs such as "Dallas". As such, these terms are sometimes also referred to as *"Dallas-Deutsch"*. Wordings such as *"nicht wirklich"* (not really), *"das macht keinen Sinn"* (that makes no sense), *"wir sehen uns später"* (see you later), *"tu es"* (do it), *"ich habe keine Idee"* (I've got no idea), *"das ist ein guter Punkt"* (that's a good point) or *"wenn ich du wäre"* (if I were you) would have sounded rather odd to a German ear just a few years ago, but now they are hardly noticed, much less smirked at. At least in this phenomenon I can take some comfort, as it means that I'm not the only one who sometimes inadvertently translates things straight out of English when speaking German.

The development of *"Doinglish"* also confuses me somewhat. After all, many English words get a whole new meaning upon their arrival: For instance, a *"Beamer"* in German is the name for a projector, a *"Handy"* is the word for mobile phone in German (though in Switzerland it is a *"Natel"*), and *"Mobbing"* in German means to bully. (I always have to smile when Germans insist that ONE person can mob another.)

In "Doinglish", a *"Freak"* is someone who is crazy about something, but not a misshapen person! Most confusing for me is German the use of *"checken"*, such as in: *"Nee, lass mal, die neue Bedeutung checke ich eh nicht"* ("No, don't worry about it; I don't get the new meaning anyway"). No-one outside of the German-speaking region is *"checking"* this meaning.

Sometimes I find the development of *"Doinglish"* to be downright appalling, for example, when the German language gets so neglected that some people even start forgetting practical German words. Often when I visit new clients at work and inquire about the location of particular departments, I am thwarted by *"Doinglish"*. For instance in conversations such as the following:

"Wo ist hier die EDV-Abteilung?"
"So was haben wir hier nicht."
"Haben Sie denn einen IT-Support?"
"Erste Etage."

And here the translation:
  "Where is the computer department?"
  "We don't have any such department here."
  "Do you have an 'IT Support'?"
  "First floor."

Another colleague of mine like to state that a law had not yet been *"live geschaltet"* ("going live"). I suspect that she meant that the law had not yet *"in Kraft getreten"* (taken effect). I then have to ask myself what you'd say in *"Doinglish"* when a law ceases to be effective. Is it then *"tot geschaltet"* ("going dead")?

Fortunately, I also think that the development of *"Doinglish"* can be funny once in a while. Foreign words often have something irresistibly exotic about them. Admittedly, sometimes they are indeed stylish, like in the case of the *"Hamburg Freezers"* (the local professional ice hockey team). The *"Hamburger Gefrierschränke"* just isn't quite as catchy ...

However, this kind of thing can also backfire. My favorite example was just around the corner from my apartment, where a building displayed the following sign in huge letters: *"ASS SECURITY."* I even took photos for evidence because I knew that, otherwise, no-one back home would believe me. The company surely wanted to be seen as *"ACE Security"*, but if so, they should have been a bit more thorough with the translation. As it was, it appeared they were just trying to cover peoples' backsides. Now, it's very possible that the company has since won over a number of customers with this marketing tactic – but probably not the type of customers they wanted...

A few years after I had recovered from this shock, I suddenly started seeing many cars throughout Hamburg that belonged to the *"Ass Team"*. (Here I also have photographic evidence!) One might conclude that over the years the word "team" has almost become a German word, but , in this case, *"Ass"* was an abbreviation for "Athletic Sport Sponsoring"! Personally, I have no desire to become a member of the *"Ass-Team"*.

The worst example of all for me, though, was the Coca Cola advertisement in Germany that claimed *"It's your Heimspiel"* ("It's your home game"). With this inconsistent sentence, the only real statement being made is that its originators didn't know how to translate *"Heimspiel"* into English. Furthermore, the Aldi Supermarket soda-pop *"Rivercola"* never fails to perplex me. I mean, I suspect that no one in Germany would ever purchase a drink called *"Flusscola"* (river-cola).

I must admit that I do sometimes have fun kidding Germans who tend to get carried away using *"Doinglish"*. Germans often do this in order to appear modern and self-confident, which is why it can be so amusing when their usage of *Doinglish* actually makes them uncertain.

For example, in the following lines are English words which Germans just can't seem to get enough of, coupled with the corresponding German word. But whenever I ask Germans why the English equivalent keeps gaining in popularity, I often just get a Teutonic shrug:

- *"Shopping & Einkaufen?"* *"Schoppen"* means shopping, but *"Frühschoppen"* pre-lunch drinking.
- "Bodyguard & Leibwächter?" The German language could really use both of these.
- *"Wellness & Wohlbefinden?"* The overuse of "Wellness" in German makes me slightly unwell.
- *"Sound & Klang?"* The meanings of the two words sound about the same to me.
- *"Button & Schaltfläche?"* I need a help-button to determine the difference.
- *"Background & Hintergrund?"* The word *"Herkunft"* (origin) also has a good background.

- *"Insider & Eingeweihter?"* Only insiders know what the difference is.
- *"Worst-case & Supergau?"* In an emergency, Germans could also say *"schlimmsten Falls"*.
- "Canceln & absagen?" Other German synonyms are *"stornieren"*, *"streichen"* or *"kündigen"*.
- *"Entführt & gekidnappt?"* Some people apparently want to kidnap the German language.

Things can get particularly ugly in *"Doinglish"* when English words are taken apart in German, for instance when the past-tense form of an English verb is made using German grammar rules, as in the case of *"upgedated"* (updated) or *"downgeloaded"* (downloaded). The *"Doinglish"* word *"gekidnappt"* seems especially misshapen to me eyes, but Germans find it quite normal. Nevertheless, even they think it odd when they hear the alternative verb form of *"kidnappiert"*.

One of my work colleagues particularly likes to use English words haphazardly in German. For example, she cheerfully kept referring to the *"Sicherheitsdienstmann"* (security guard) as *"der Security Guard"*, even though he looked quintessentially German and couldn't speak English at all. At some point I asked her why she did this. She enthusiastically answered: "It just sounds more international!"

In the German business world, the word *"Kickoff-meeting"* is becoming more and more popular, even though no-one really knows what it means. Once, while at a difficult client's office, I made a joke in German along the lines of, "I hope this isn't going to become a 'Kickout-meeting'!" Suddenly I was surrounded by confused expressions on all of the Germans' faces.

Evidently, some Germans are with me in thinking that *"Doinglish"* is getting a little out of hand. For instance my friend Petra, who has even joined the *"Verein Deutsche Sprache"*

(*"VdS"* for short), a club founded to protect the German language. Despite her commitment to this cause, she often seems not to notice that she herself actually often does lots of *"Doinglish-ing"*. For example, when I asked her about how things were going in the club, she apparently didn't notice the irony of her response, *"Es is nicht so **easy**, immer bei den **Meetings** dabei zu sein, da die mir vom **Timing** her oft nicht passen"* ("It's not that easy always making it to the meetings because the timing is often just not right for my schedule.") In the meantime, I have almost come to the conclusion that nowadays only native English speakers can speak "pure" German. This claim may not seem to make much sense at first, but this is easy to explain: In our German courses, our grades inevitably suffered each time we included English words and terms in our German sentences!

I am aware that English's "non-hostile-takeover" hasn't only been occurring in Germany. English is actually becoming increasingly important in just about every country on the planet. Ironically enough, though, one of the few exceptions is the USA, where Spanish is gaining in importance.

Of course, this development is even more confusing for the people in Germany who have never learned English. The grandmother of a friend of mine was so frustrated by an advertisement by the *'Deutschen Bahn'* (German rail system), that she wrote a letter to their management complaining about how she had counted sixteen English words in a short "German" text, resulting in her not being able to understand the contents. After waiting a long time in vain for an answer to her letter, she then personally drove to the respective management center in order to give the persons responsible a good piece of her mind. The manager told her that, nowadays, the company has to show that it is "international" and "open to the world". Her reply: "If you want to show real openness to the world, then you should put up two versions: one in German and one in English. No one can understand a mishmash of the two!" Respect, Grandma! With such a clear and straightforward statement, I can imagine that the *Deutsche Bahn* manager "felt a bad feeling".

Maybe I am just envious that Germans can adorn their sentences with so many words borrowed from English. After all, sometimes I'd love to pep up my English conversations with some particularly practical German words. Although, then it perhaps could be said that "The English language is being *'entführted'*."

How does that sound?

24: Chewing through the German CH-Sound

Similarly to how the pronunciation of the English TH can trip up many German tongues, the German CH can become a real tongue-twister for native English speakers. If German and English are linguistic relatives, then these sounds are the black sheep of the family.

My grammar book stated matter-of-factly that the pronunciation of the German CH is similar to the way Scots pronounce the English word "loch". Unfortunately, this description is not very helpful for most Americans, since this Scottish pronunciation is even more mysterious than the "Loch Ness Monster" itself.

Up until my special pronunciation sessions with Frau Güllicher at the Goethe-Institut, I always pronounced the German CH in exactly the same manner: in the back of my mouth. Of course, Frau Güllicher considered this sub-optimal. "Herr Bergmann, that is how the Swiss do it. Not that I have anything against the Swiss, but that is not good." She then proceeded to explain to me the two pronunciation possibilities of the CH in German. The CH-sound is only to be pronounced in the back of the mouth, so to speak out of the throat, when it follows the vowels A, O and U. Otherwise, it is to be pronounced in the front of the mouth, in other words, following the vowels Ä, ÄU, E, EI, Ö or Ü. This is why the CH in *"Güllicher"* sounds so very different than in *"Aussprachebuch"*.

Frau Güllicher gave me the impression that, after such an explanation, everything should now be crystal clear for me. But I still had questions:

- My question: "How do you pronounce the CH, when it follows a D, as in ‚*Mädchen*?"

Her answer: "In the front of the mouth, as in the word *,ich'.*"

- My question: "And what do you do when it follows the letter S, as in *,pfuschen*?"
  Her answer: "Just like in the English SH-sound."
- My question: "But what about *,matschig*?"

For the first time, Frau Güllicher needed to ponder for a few seconds before replying: "Then it is like in the English word *,Match'.*" But I did not give up so easily, and I asked her how a person would pronounce the following exercise from my grammar book: *"Ein chaotischer Chilene zweifelhaften Charakters baute ein charmantes Chalet mit einem chamois Dach chinesischen Stils in Chemnitz."* („A chaotic Chilean of dubious character built a charming chalet with a chamois roof in the Chinese-style in Chemnitz.") Her response: "That depends on where the person grew up in Germany." With these words, she pushed me in the direction of the door. As a result, I did not get a chance to pose any further questions, such as whether the peculiar way in which the Swiss pronounce the CH is the real reason is why Switzerland is often abbreviated as "CH".

In contrast to Frau Güllicher, most Germans are not even aware that there are two possible ways to pronounce the CH in German. When I took a beginning Swedish course in Göttingen in the fall of 1996, the Germans in the class complained loudly about certain consonants in Swedish having varying pronunciations, depending upon the vowel preceded them. The normally very placid teacher became slightly nervous in the face of uproar. At least until I went into action by announcing that this was actually the exact same rule as for the German-CH. In spite of my numerous contributions to the general success of the class, my popularity among the Germans in the class seemed to decline daily.

After one semester in Göttingen, I thought that I had more or less mastered the pronunciation of the German CH-sound. But then I moved to *"Hamburch"*, where the natives say *"Guten Tach"* instead of *"Guten Tag"*. It is often stated that the "purest" German is spoken in Hannover. At first, I did not really notice any linguistic differences between the cities with the license plates beginning with "HH" and "H" respectively. As a result, I started thinking that I also had acquired a "pure" German pronunciation. But then I received a letter addressed to a certain "Herr Berchmann". It had come from a southern German businessman with whom I had only had contact over the telephone. Evidently, my pronunciation had become somewhat *"frachlich"*. Unfortunately, the path back to a correct pronunciation of the German G-sound was going to be somewhat *"schwierich"* for me, since the German G sometimes sounds like a CH, but also sometimes not. (At the end of syllables such as in "schwierig" it sounds like a CH, but not at the end of syllables such as in "fraglich" or "Bergmann".)

Although my German became progressively better over time in Hamburg, I still had problems with words such as *"Streiktaktik"* (strike-tactic), *"hektisch"* (hectic) and *"Technik"* (technique). These I tended to mispronounce as *"Streichtachtich"*, *"hechtisch"* and *"Technich"*. This was evidently due to a certain over-compensation on my part. While speaking a foreign language, one is sometimes so preoccupied by trying to avoid overlooking any of the foreign sounds, that one implements them even when they are out of place. In this way, I solved the riddle which has mystified native English speaker for ages: Why do Germans tend to replace the English V-sound with the English W-sound? Even many Germans who speak English brilliantly nevertheless sometimes speak of *"Willages"* instead of Villages, *"Wideos"* instead of "Videos" and *"Wegetables"* instead of "Vegetables". And the German language doesn't even have the English W-sound! I found the solution in *"Hamburch"*: In this respect, the Germans are simply too *"fleißich"*! ("hard-working")

***

In March 1997, not only was my ability to discern between the various German CH-forms in danger, but also the security of my abode in the country. The end of my internship not only entailed a full-time contract, along with a moderate raise in salary, but also the end of my time in the furnished studio for interns. To my regret, remaining in the studio was not an option, considering that the monthly rent was way out of my league. In fact, it was higher than the rent had been for my entire five-month stay in Frau Wilbärt's "broom-closet" apartment in Göttingen. And my company only paid the rent of the studio as long as I was officially an intern. Suddenly, I missed the good old lady, apart from her landlady laughter, of course.

As soon as my new full-time contract was in my hands, I headed once again for a telephone booth in order to begin my search for an apartment. As usual, fortune did not strike until I called an older lady who had a furnished room for rent. Even though she did not pick me up with her car at the telephone booth, the room seemed suitable for me. Within a very short amount of time, Frau Lülläu became like a sister to me – but unfortunately not like a sister of mine, but rather like a sister of Frau Wilbärt. The similarities between the two of them were rather striking ...

The apartment was a very beautiful *"Altbauwohnung"* (apartment from before World War I) in the chic neighborhood of Eppendorf, not far from *"Klosterstern"* (a traffic circle translatable as "cloister -star"). Unfortunately, the house-rules were stricter than in a cloister. Since the apartment was gigantic, several of the rooms were rented out. Next to me lived a businessman, and in the next room over lived a woman whom I never saw – Frau Lülläu must have trained her well in the meantime…

We flat mates only shared the kitchen, the hallway and the bathroom. The bathroom was a tricky subject. Should a tenant linger there too long, it was likely that Frau Lülläu would show up soon with a pointed finger and a pointed remark such as: *"Machen Sie sich schnell fertig, oder ich mache Sie fertig!"* (Finish up quickly, or I'll finish you off.") The only thing that she seemed to really wanted to share with us was a piece of her mind. Now and then Frau Lülläu found a hair in the shower – one of mine. Of course, this caused me to come within a hair's breadth of getting thrown out of the apartment!

Actually, Frau Lülläu could also be somewhat gracious. One day in May, she even invited me to drink a glass of red wine with her. The occasion was the visit of one of her relatives from a village on the outskirts of Hamburg. Even though this rural relative was only indirectly related to Frau Lülläu, she could be very direct with me, and she asked me all sorts of probing questions. First of all, she wanted to know if I had a university degree. I replied that, not only had I studied, but my studies had also cost sixty thousand dollars. I must admit, I was not prepared for her follow-up question: "Did all of the students have to pay so much, or only you?"

Then she asked me what my profession was. I was unsure what the best translation of "Certified Public Accountant" into German should be, since – strictly speaking – I was not after all a German *"Wirtschaftsprüfer"*. So I replied: *"Ich bin Buchhalter."* (I am a bookkeeper.) She did not even try to hide her disappointment when she said: "Herr Bergmann, you studied four years and paid thousands and thousands of dollars just to become a *'Erbsenzähler'?* (bean counter)" Because I was not quite sure at the time what a *"Erbsen-zähler"* was, I answered yes. It was all too obvious that my response did not impress her in the least. Somewhat red in the face, I decided to throw caution into the wind, and I exclaimed: "I mean, I'm a *'Wirtschaftsprüfer'!*" By her expression I noted that this was perhaps sometime too flattering a translation. She summarized: "Herr Bergmann, *'Wirtschaftsprüfer'* are like dentists: somewhat painful, but also often necessary. Though not generally popular, they cannot be avoided. But, be that as it may, a person is proud to have one in the family."

In spite of that, neither the rural-relative nor Frau Lülläu were exactly sure what a *"Wirtschaftsprüfer"* actually does. Unfortunately, I also could not explain it to them in concise and understandable terms. Later that evening, I pondered what the best way would be to explain to laypersons my profession in German. When I read in a magazine for auditors how corporate sharks *"Unternehmen übernehmen"*, (take-over undertakings), the following summary occurred to me: "As a lawyer, one must *"unter Zeugen überzeugen"* (convince among witnesses), as a soldier *"unter Fallen überfallen"* (attack among traps), as an investment advisor *"unter Weisen überweisen"* (transfer money among wisemen) – and as a Wirtschaftsprüfer one must *"unter Listen überlisten"* (outwit among lists).

The next day a colleague of mine explained to me exactly just how much longer and more demanding the *"Wirtschaftsprüfer"* title is compared with the corresponding American CPA. I considered whether I should explain this to Frau Lülläu's rural-relative, but then I thought: *"Was sie nicht weiß, macht MICH nicht heiß"*. ("What she doesn't know won't hurt me.")

When it came to passing along telephone messages, Frau Lülläu was not very precise, since she did not like writing things of that sort down on paper. So it was not unheard of for her to say things to me along the following lines upon my arrival home from work: "Herr Bergmann, someone called for you. I don't remember who it was, but it was important, and you are supposed to call back." On the other hand, she was not at all hesitant to let me know her opinion about me. "Herr Bergmann, I don't like your American accent, neither when you speak German nor when you speak English. British English is much, much better."

Even though she often stated that one should not be *"päpstlicher als der Papst"* (Popelier than the Pope), this evidently did not prevent her from being "queenlier than the Queen" when it came to the English language. Fortunately, I knew how to defend myself in such a situation. I replied: "I know exactly what you mean, Frau Lülläu: I have to come terms somehow with your not having a beautiful Swiss accent in German."

In reality, I like many of the various German accents, but I truly do like the sound of German spoken by the Swiss the best. And, of course, I wanted to annoy Frau Lülläu just a little bit. At that time I had met several nice people at the university, of which one was a Swiss man by the name of Bodo. Bodo had just started on his doctoral thesis encompassing the comparison and deciphering of various incomplete mediaeval manuscripts in Latin. All of these were themselves, in turn, a duplicate of an even older manuscript. Bodo's mission was, therefore, to ascertain how the original manuscript must have looked. It was also his goal to finish the doctoral thesis before he himself was middle-aged.

In Bodo's institute there were PhD students from all over Europe, most of whom came from Italy or Greece. Although these students were very different, they all had one thing in common: They were all of the opinion that Bodo spoke the most melodious sounding German. Therefore, it was incomprehensible to us that Bodo himself did not like to discuss this topic. He seemed to just want to blend into the linguistic background in Hamburg. That is why he reacted so annoyedly when a cute student at a party wanted to pay him a compliment on account of his accent. To quote Bodo: "The fastest way to turn a Swiss into an enemy is to imitate his accent!" I, on the other hand, behaved much more amiably towards the student, but she unfortunately seemed to find my American accent decidedly less appealing…

In June 1997, Bodo and I travelled with five students from the Aiesec Program of the Hamburg University to Amsterdam. Once there, Bodo and I headed out in search of museums which had nothing to do with modern art. In the meantime, the five other students started straight off in search of "Marihuana-Muffins". Unfortunately, the chef in one of the appropriate cafés must have munched on one muffin too many before his shift… My evidence? Approximately thirty minutes after the five students had eaten up the last of the crumbs, four of them complained bitterly about not feeling a thing. However, the fifth one lay on the ground, where she eloquently and succinctly described her feelings on the subject as follows: "I am dying."

At that time, Bodo lived in a somewhat dingy dormitory behind an insane-asylum in northern Hamburg. These living arrangements may not have been exactly what he wanted, but he could not afford his own apartment on account of his rather modest stipendium. In the summer of 1997 Bodo therefore asked me if I would like to set up a *"Wohngemeinschaft"* (a "shared-flat", or *"WG"* for short) with him. According to Bodo, ours would be a *"WG"* where peace reigns in the WC and people don't get in each other's hair. I could imagine that we would fit together well, since even by Swiss standards I am very orderly. In Switzerland, after all, orderliness is next to Godliness. Or as Bodo liked to put it. *"In der Schweiz wird selten etwas verbaselt."* (In Switzerland nothing gets lost.)

And so, even though autumn was approaching, the thoughts of a friendly apartment in *"Hamburch"* caused it to feel like springtime in my heart.

25: On a Scale of "So la la" to "Ooh la la!"

Even if the English language continues to tighten its grip on the inhabitants of the German-speaking countries, the French have not yet given up in their guerilla warfare against English-language world-domination. At a university party in Hamburg I met a formidable Frenchwoman by the name of Claire. Right from the start, Claire made it very clear to me that she had an aversion towards the USA. But I could take some comfort in the knowledge that other countries also did not escape her ire. For instance, evidently the French weren't about to forgive and forget the Hundred Years War after a mere five centuries when it came to England. Moreover, the Belgians were supposedly dimwitted, the Swiss too wealthy, and the Italians too friendly (especially to non-French-people). And when it came to the Germans, an amiable attitude was out of the question after three very poor showings in the latest wars with them.

Out of curiosity, I asked Claire whether there was any country on the globe which the French actually liked. But once I saw how her lips began forming a Q, I quickly added: "Apart from Quebec!" Several minutes later she somewhat hesitatingly admitted: "We kind of like Sweden..." After she had spoken at length in glowing terms about tall, strong, blonde Swedish men, I began regretting having ever posed the question.

Claire considered the recent development in the use of foreign words in German to be most disagreeable. As she explained it: "A *"Chef"* has become a *"Boss"*, a *"Bankier"* is now a "Banker", a *"Fusion"* is called a "Merger", an *"Etikett"* is labeled a *"Label"*, a *"Fete"* has become a *"Party"* and a *"Jour fixe"* is referred to as a *"Daily Meeting"*. Worst of all, however, French is now not even called '*passé*', by Germans, but rather *"out"!*" To be honest, Claire was actually a very lovely woman, and she liked foreign languages a lot, but I shall never forget her reaction upon hearing that in German French is classified as an "Indo-GERMANIC language". (In other languages this category is called "Indo-European".)

As is the case with many French native-speakers, Claire also had some slight problems with German pronunciation. This was perhaps most evident when she once said: *"Oh la la, ein großer Affengeburtstag!"* ("Oh la la, a big monkey birthday!" – She had meant to say *"Hafen"* (harbor), but instead it sounded like *"Affen"* (monkey).) For many French-speakers, the letter H is indeed silent but deadly, something that Germans find to be "orribly" funny. In order to placate Claire, Petra said to her: "Ah, Claire, don't worry. You have an elegant and charming accent." Eavesdropping on this *"Tête-à-Tête"*, I glanced over at Petra with child-like innocence in my eyes and tugged at her sleeve. She gave me an understanding, yet uncompromising, look and stated: "David, yours is neither elegant nor charming. At most, it is perhaps cool." At least that's something!

In our search for our very own domicile, Bodo and I started looking in the newspaper adverts. There I quickly noticed that I had to be on my toes whenever I saw something with a touch of "French-ness". Evidently, Germans like trying to conceal anything unpleasant with a whiff of French elegance. (In other words: if it sounds like *"Oh la la"* then it is often instead only *"so la la"*.) The best example of this is the word *"Courtage"* (agent-comission). In good German it could just as easily be called *"Maklerprovision"*, but then it would sound as painful as it actually is. After all, for many apartments in Hamburg, all the agent has to do is simply open the door and then let the huge commission flow from the new tenants into his bank-account.

Further examples of euphemisms which inspire very little euphoria in tenants:

- *"französischer Balkon"*: Only tiny feet fit on such a little balcony.
- *"Maisonette"*: A whole lot of ups and downs.
- *"Hochparterre"*: More or less on street level.
- *"Parterre"*: Almost in the basement.
- *"Souterrain"*: In the basement.

After a few hours with the newspaper, it seemed fairly clear to me that in Hamburg the subject of balconies is an important one. For instance, it is always emphasized in adverts whether an apartment has a south-west-balcony. It is common knowledge that Muslims in Europe search for a spot facing the southeast where they can worship in the direction of Mecca. Less well known is the fact that Christians in Germany evidently prefer their very own pleasant spot outdoors facing the southwest, so that they can better "worship" the "sun-god".

Bodo and I looked at several apartments over the course of a few weeks. The saddest experiences for us were the apartments which we were interested in, but which were not interested in us. At some of the better apartments, we simply were drowned out by the sea of applicants. At some of the less desirable apartments, we made it further along, but then were turned down by the landlords who gave us varying reasons for their rejection of our applications: Some did not want to rent their apartment to two men, others did not want any foreigners, (even if they considered us – as a Swiss-German and North-American – to belong to the "good" category of foreigners). But what I absolutely did not understand at first was why some landlords did not want us because we supposedly looked too much like a teacher and a lawyer … (I discovered later that these are two of the least desired professions of tenants in Germany, due to their tendency to be all too willing to put their knowledge to uncooperative purposes.)

Finally, Bodo resolved to place an advert himself in the newspaper. He wrote: "PhD student and CPA, both gainfully employed, looking for a three-room apartment." Already the very next day a landlady called to offer to show us a suitable apartment. I never would have thought that it could be so easy! It did not bother us that the somewhat run-down apartment was not very homey at first – we nevertheless right away felt right at home.

What I then quickly realized was that when an apartment in Germany is classified as "unfurnished", then it is really and truly "unfurnished". In the USA there is usually at least a refrigerator in the kitchen and a few light bulbs hanging from the ceiling. But in Germany there seem to be nothing inside apart from perhaps a few lonely tumble-weeds tumbling about.

To rectify the situation, Bodo proposed that we drive to IKEA. At first I was not sure why we would want to take a vacation there. (On account of several highway exit signs, I was namely of the opinion that IKEA must be a suburb or city somewhere.) But Bodo explained that IKEA is a furniture store. It may be a world-wide company, but in the 90's it had not yet really caught on in the USA, so I had not heard of it, in contrast to apparently every single German alive. Not many Germans realize that no other country in the world has as many IKEA stores as Germany!

At IKEA, not only does one encounter loads of reasonably priced pieces of furniture with quirky names containing numerous umlauts, but also countless arguing couples. German couples tend to live a lot longer in apartments together "in sin" than Americans do. During my first visit to an IKEA, several things became clear to me. Instead of an engagement period, couples in Germany evidently undergo a *"Pärchenkompatibilitätstest"* („test of couple-compatibility") which consists of the following: They drive on a Saturday together to an IKEA, where they engage in epic struggles with both each other and a few hundred other couples in order to obtain various low-value-items. The decision of which objects to buy and how to squeeze more of them than the law actually allows into a car, and then later to assemble them piece by piece into recognizable furniture is evidently the German "test of couple-compatibility". If the relationship survives IKEA, then there is clearly no stopping it until death does it part.

Shortly after Bodo and I had moved into the apartment, the nosey neighbor from the apartment below us, Herr Ähinger, stopped on by. He wanted to point out that the building was "*hellhörig*". The word "*hellhörig*" immediately left a big impression upon me, since we don't have such a vivid equivalent in English. The closest I have been able to come up with is "poorly soundproofed", which is clearly less colorful than the literal translation of "*hellhörig*„: (" bright-hearable").

My experience has shown that there are the following levels of "sound-proofedness" in German:
- *"Totenstill"* (deathly quiet) The apartment is worth its weight in gold.
- *"Dunkelhörig"* ("darkly" quiet) The apartment is ok.
- *"Hörig"* (to be a slave to) This is a topic for a different sort of book …
- "*Hellhörig*" ("bright-hearable") The apartment is too loud.
- *"Höllehörig"* ("hellishly" hearable) Ouch!
- *"ellörig"* Claire's apartment.

Herr Ähinger's first visit was unfortunately not to be his last. Supposedly, we had soon thereafter given him cause to stop by in order to instruct us on the "inviolability" of the *Ruhezeiten* ("Quiet-Hours"). In the following weeks, Bodo and I noted that the 45-year-old, unemployed window-washer, on account of his unemployment, had relatively large amounts of time to dedicate himself to his hobbies: shaving, not shaving, bossing his wife around, and bossing his wife's dog around. His motto evidently was: *"Immer mit der Ruhe!"* ("Take it easy!"; but literally "Always with the quiet!")

Herr Ähinger was especially proud of his business acumen. After all, he had discovered that he could earn more through unemployment-compensation and some side-jobs than he could through working officially. For some unfathomable reason, however, he obviously did not seem to appreciate my paying considerable contributions into the German social security system, thereby facilitating his life of ease. At first, Bodo and I tried to be on friendly terms with him, but we quickly learned that it was not a good idea to inquire how the job search was going. Apparently, it had not been going well since the beginning of the Helmut-Kohl-Administration. Kohl came into power in 1982 ...

This unwelcome guest introduced me to several indecipherable gestures. Fortunately, Bodo was able to interpret the mysterious signals and thereby enlighten me. "When Herr Ähinger holds his hand slightly cupped facing his neck, and states that he has *,so einen Hals'* ('such a neck'), it does not mean that he has a sore throat, but rather that he is upset. When he screams that he has *,die Nase voll'* (,the nose full'), it does not mean that he has a cold, but rather than he is really fed up." I listened intently to Bodo as he continued: "Whenever Herr Ähinger taps his pointer finger against the side of his head, it does not mean that he has a headache, but rather that he is certain that he is *'doch nicht blöd'* ('not stupid')" And that wasn't all, Bodo went on further: "When he says that *"ihm der Kragen platzt"* ('his collar is going to burst'), it does not mean that he had eaten too much, but rather that he is furious. Concluding, Bodo explained, "And when he waves his open hand in front of his face, it does not mean that he is blind, but rather that he believes that someone else is blind."

Herr Ähinger's part-time job, which he performed free of charge, was to ensure that someone should thunder at us should we make the slightest peep during the "Quiet Hours". Up until then, I had not been familiar with the concept of such a quiet time, since we don't have such a thing where I grew up in the USA. But I quickly became aware that in Germany the "Quiet Hours" last from 1:00 pm until 3:00 pm and from 10:00 pm until 7:00 am. At first, I thought this meant that one should not have wild parties during that time. But our neighbor stopped on by every time when we vacuum cleaned, washed the laundry or took a shower. Moreover, since the entire Sunday is a "Quiet Day", I was afraid that we would be getting an unpleasant visit after every Sunday shower. After all, it looked as if Herr Ähinger was of the opinion that daily showering was completely overrated...

Fortunately, after a short time of troubles we were able to conclude a neighborly peace agreement: We would accept it when he got loud, for instance by turning up his stereo on Fridays (in order to celebrate a hard week of not-working), or when he loudly woke up his wife in the mornings (with classics such as *"Ich hab Hunger, Hunger, Hunger! Aufstehen und Essen holen!"* – "I'm hungry, hungry, hungry! Get up and get food!"). He, on the other hand, would tolerate it when I cleaned certain things during the "Quiet-Hours", for instance myself.

We also had to promise Herr Ähinger that we would remove our ancient washing-machine. Bodo and I at least saw the sense in this. After all, its spin-cycle sent the entire building into convulsions. Although the apartment may have been unfurnished in the beginning, one solitary object did stand there when we moved in. However, this was probably not due to any magnanimity on the part of the previous tenants, but rather to the fact that the washing machine seemed to weigh more than a tow-truck. Moreover, we felt a nagging suspicion that the German Green Party, which had recently come into power, would soon be talking to us about the impact that our washing machine was having on the nature preserves on the outskirts of Hamburg.

Not only Herr Ähinger and the animals of the slightly-shaken nature-preserves were happy about our new washing machine. Bodo and I were also thrilled. Our new acquisition clearly had not been given the brandname of *"Meisterstück"* (masterpiece) for nothing. In contrast to most American washing machines, which are top-loading, ours was a typical, small, efficient front-loader which was frugal with energy and water. During a bargain-hunt, we succeeded in rounding up this lucky-buy at a special offer at the Karstadt store nearby. We couldn't turn it down, most of all because the offer not only included cheap delivery, but also the free picking up and disposal of our old washing machine. This was a deal-clincher.

In spite of my relief, I was overcome with a guilty conscience when I watched how the three men from the Karstadt-delivery service heaved our old monster out of the apartment. The first man complained that he was paid to transport washing machines, not safes. The second man asked whether we had perhaps washed lots of stones over the years. And the third contributed to my blossoming vocabulary of swear words in German.

And thus my first year in Germany drew to a close. Now, I may not yet have become a *"große Nummer"* ("big cheese"; literally "big number") in the land of my forefathers, but at least I was well on my way to becoming what the Germans refer to as a *"08/15-ausländischer-Mitbürger"* (run-of-the-mill foreign citizen)!

26: Auf Wiedergucken

In German there are many possible ways of saying goodbye. Unfortunately, at the Goethe-Institut in Chicago we basically focused on *"Auf Wiedersehen"* – something which I rarely ever hear in everyday life in Germany. Instead, I usually hear expressions like: *"Bis nachher", "Man sieht sich", "Bis dann", "Lebe wohl", "Mach's gut", "Bis die Tage", "Wir sehen uns", "Bis bald", "Ciao", "Bis demnächst", "Tschüß", "Bis spatter", "Tschüßi",* "Bis dahin" or even *"Bye-bye"*. And after telephone conversations, I often hear an extremely quickly spoken: *"Alsobisspäterwirhörenvoneinandertschüüüüß!"* (Ok-see-you-later-we'll-hear-from-each-other-byyyyyyyeeeee!)

Choosing the appropriate form for each situation is not always so easy for non-native German speakers as just saying *"Auf Wiedersehen"* would be. For instance, it is not correct, as I had falsely assumed for years, to always say *"Bis später"* (till later). (This is in contrast to American English where it is almost always possible to say "see you later".) It also took some time before I realized that one should not say *"Lebe wohl!"* (farewell) to everyone, as in most cases this more or less means: *"Auf Nimmerwiedersehen!"* (Until we never meet again!) Moreover, it wasn't until after getting several nasty looks that I noticed that in the southern parts of the German speaking world, one should only say *"tschüß!"* („ciao") to close acquaintances. However, there one could say *"Ciao, Bella!"*, but only if one looks like Don Juan – something which I unfortunately do not.

But everything must come to an end sooner or later. And if there is one thing that one is not allowed to be when parting ways in German, it is to be at a loss for words. In order to make the ending of this book happy, I would like to conclude with several words I have made up which I believe could make the

German language EVEN MORE humorous:

- *"demuttiviert"* – What a grown man becomes who has to move out from his *"Mutti"* (Mommy).
- *"Mampframsch"* – (chow-trash) With this new German word, who needs the term "Junkfood"?
- *"stehkrank"* – (standing-sick) What a person without a seat reservation can get on the ICE-Train.
- *"Danebenbuhler"* – A *"Nebenbuhler"* (rival) who always falls short (*daneben*).
- *"Frauenmissversteher"* – (Women-misunderstanders) What many male *"Danebenbuhler"* are.
- *"entdoofen"* – (to "de-silly") To alter something so that it is no longer *"doof"* (silly).
- „*Plattmachmobil*" – (flattening-mobile) A much more vivid description than *"Panzer"* (tank).
- *"Partypate"* – (party-godfather) A tad cooler than just being a *"Salonlöwe"* (socialite).
- *"Mitternachtsmuffel"* – (midnight-slouch) Something a *"Partypate"* never is.
- *"Wannewonne"* – (bathtub-bliss) The wonderful feeling in one's own bathtub.
- *"tatensatt"* – (action-satiated) When one no longer feels a driving urge to do things.
- *"Boxenstoppstelle"* – Where even manly men can proverbially "powder their noses".
- *"memmenmäßig"* – (coward-like) The way a scaredy-cat behaves.
- *"hasenclever"* – (bunny-clever) And why not actually?

But even if it isn't always possible to be *"hasenclever"*, one should at least know – as the Germans like to say – where *"der Hase lang läuft"* (which way the wind is blowing; literally "where the hare is running") or whether he *"im Pfeffer liegt"* (where the crux of the matter is; literally "whether he is lying the in pepper").

Over the years, many Germans have asked me what it is like to learn to speak German as a foreign language. I summarize it as follows: "It's like driving a BMW 7-Series on the ice: You are definitely aware of having something powerful at your disposal, but somehow you just can't seem to get it completely under control."

I hope that this book successfully convinces more people that German is indeed an underestimated language. And I would be pleased to hear the following much more often: *"Mensch, das war ja witzig! Typisch Deutsch eben!"* (Man, that was funny! Typically German, so to speak!)

Thanks:
No book is written alone, and this book has been no exception.
I would like to take this opportunity to send out a big "Thank You"
to the following people who have supported me in this endeavor,
either directly or indirectly:

Inke Myschker, Joe Bergman, Almut von Bodelschwingh,
Sarah Brackbill, Johannes und Monika Enneking, Tom Fussell,
Nicole Göbel, Tanja Güllicher, Inken Hahnemann, Olaf Hille,
Hartmut Karottki, Sharon und Jeff Krietemeyer, Anja Lauterbach,
Chapin Landvogt, Terry McDonagh, Charles Mescher, Natalie Molter,
Daniela Müller, Bodo Näf, Angela Rosin, Annika Siems.

MORE BLAUPAUSE BOOKS:

Terry McDonagh: IN THE LIGHT OF BRIDGES. HAMBURG FRAGMENTS

Paperback / 132 pages / ISBN 978-3-933498-16-8 / € 12.00

This book is not a city handbook – it is much, much more: it's the poetic journey of an Irish poet in his adopted city.
"*In the Light of Bridges* is a bittersweet love song to Hamburg. Terry McDonagh is a master bard of the home from home; integrated he may be, but 'tidy and tailored', as he claims here? Never. He has an observing novelist's eye for the specifics of place and anempathetic poet's ear for the universality of the human spirit. He is a writer with a sharp nib and a generous heart."

(Ian Watson, editor of **new***leaf* magazine)

Terry McDonagh: B O X E S

Paperback / 64 pages / ISBN 978-3-933498-12-0 / € 10.00

In this highly original and very exciting poetry for young people, Terry McDonagh has not forgotten what it's like to be young.
The poems are about the really important things in life that children see with such honesty. It is a world of daydreams and wonder, but also about misfits like 'Tone Deaf Peter' who are happy to sing their own song. McDonagh's poetry will make you laugh, celebrate silliness and remember the freedom that comes with imagination. The poetry is like a sweet revenge on all those who love rules for their own sake …
Geoffrey Gates (Australian author of 'A Ticket for Perpetual Locomotion)

McDonagh certainly keeps the bardic tradition of Mayo to the fore in all of his poetry. Above all else, the humour in this intelligent collection, Boxes, rises like cream to the top.
Colette Nic Aodha (Inis, The Irish Literary Magazine)

Terry McDonagh, Sally McKenna (Illustrations): CILL AODÁIN & NOWHERE ELSE

Hardcover / 72 pages / ISBN 978-3-933498-33-5 / € 20.00

Terry McDonagh, a native of Cill Aodáin, has lived abroad for many years. *I set out from this place*. His poetry describes his experience of the familiar, but from the viewpoint of a person whose vision has been enriched by distance.
Sally McKenna, on the other hand, is an American and more than a native. Her art work reflects the passionate attachment she has developed for the countryside and population of this part of Ireland.
This collaborative work pays a moving and graphic tribute to the region; its colour, history, and people first described by the blind bard, Raftery.
The twenty-eight poems and pictures are rich, meditative, passionate and lyrical. They sweep through the fields, along the bog road and into the hearts of men, women and children who have given Cill Aodáin its human face.

www.umlauts.eu

www.derdiewas.de

www.blaupause-books.com